DATE DUE

Demco

FOLK TREASURES OF MEXICO

FOLK TREASURES

The Nelson A. Rockefeller Collection
in the San Antonio Museum of Art and the Mexican Museum, San Francisco

OF MEXICO

Text by Marion Oettinger, Jr.

With foreword by Ann Rockefeller Roberts and photographs by Lee Boltin

Additional photographs by John Dyer and captions and photographs by Annie O'Neill

Arte Público Press
Houston, Texas

Folk art has in it the pulse beat of the human hand.

—*Pál Kelemen, Vanishing Art of the Americas, 1977*

Editor: Gabriela Baeza Ventura
Designer: Dana Sloan

On page i:
Negrito Mask. Michoacán. San Antonio Museum of Art
(detail of Plate 59)

On pages ii–iii:
Teodora Blanco. **Animal Band.** Oaxaca. Mexican Museum,
San Francisco, and San Antonio Museum of Art (Plate 86)

Note of the plate captions:
The abbreviations MM and SAMA stand for the Mexican
Museum, San Francisco, and the San Antonio Museum of
Art, respectively.

Folk Treasures of Mexico: The Nelson A. Rockefeller Collection is made
possible through grants from Ann Rockefeller Roberts and the City
of Houston through the Houston Arts Alliance.

Recovering the past, creating the future

Arte Público Press
University of Houston
452 Cullen Performance Hall
Houston, Texas 77204-2004

Cover design by Dana Sloan

Oettinger, Jr., Marion.
   Folk Treasures of Mexico: The Nelson A. Rockefeller Collection
/ by Marion Oettinger, Jr.; photographs by Lee Boltin.
      p.   cm.
Originally published: New York: Abrams, 1990.
Includes bibliographical references and index.
ISBN 978-1-55885-595-3 (alk. paper)
   1. Folk art—Mexico. 2. Rockefeller, Nelson A. (Nelson Aldrich)
1908-1979—Art collections. 3. Folk art—Private collections—
New York (State)—New York. I. Boltin, Lee. II. San Antonio
Museum of Art. III. Mexican Museum. IV. Title.
NK844.O35 2010
745.0972'07473—dc22
                                                    2009053981
                                                    CIP

♾ The paper used in this publication meets the requirements of the
American National Standard for Information Sciences—Permanence of
Paper for Printed Library Materials, ANSI Z39.48-1984.

Printed in China
February 2010–May 2010
Creative Printing USA Inc.
12 11 10 9 8 7 6 5 4 3 2 1

Contents

Foreword by Ann Rockefeller Roberts

t brings great joy and satisfaction to introduce the second edition of *Folk Treasures of Mexico. The Nelson A. Rockefeller Collection.* What is most exciting is that this wonderful book will once again be available to scholars and lovers of Mexican folk art. Equally important is Father's original dream of having the book published in Spanish and English so that the people whose genius and loving celebration of life who brought forth this infinitely varied and engaging art will have access to it in their own language.

Marion Oettinger, Jr., the author of the original text, has once again graciously consented to put pen to paper and written a fine Prologue that eloquently describes what has happened to the Mexican Folk Art collections at SAMA (San Antonio Museum of Art) during the intervening nineteen years. The readers thus are brought into the present and told of the remarkable accomplishments that have taken place in this time. It is a great story that tells of the dedication, creativity and untiring efforts of the staff; of the wonderful generosity of loyal board members, donors and volunteers who continue to give of their time, skills and funds; and of how inspiring the collections are. All of this has brought forth the magic that wants to be known, shared and enjoyed. It infuses the air in the galleries with the color, motion, humor and pathos of life itself. The objects are accessible to young and old alike and all those in between. They remind us of our own stories, our personal celebrations, our foibles. We leave the galleries feeling lighter, smiling, perhaps even with the desire to make a celebration of our own.

It has taken some time to bring forth this new edition, and every step of the way has been guided by those who believed in the project and were ready and willing to assist. As a result, the process has been an important collaboration among many people.

To begin, Henry A. J. Ramos, Executive Editor of the Hispanic Civil Rights Series at Arte Público Press, worked closely with me to create a plan that detailed what was required for republication, and gave his confidence and support throughout. He introduced me to Nicolás Kanellos, Director of Arte Público Press at the University of Houston, and things began to move.

Nicolás agreed to take on this complex project of republishing a second edition and a Spanish edition concurrently. Since then he and Gabriela Baeza Ventura, Executive Editor at APP, have personally overseen and directed every aspect of the process with great skill and personal commitment in a remarkably short time. Nicolás also brought Artes de México Press to publish the Spanish edition. As he noted, they not only accepted the project but put it as a priority in their publishing schedule creating an entirely new book for Spanish-language readers. Their enthusiasm, dedication and expert translation has resulted in a timely completion of this book for Spanish-speakers.

Annie O'Neill, who was an important contributor to the first edition as folklorist, photographer and caption writer, rejoined us. This time, she single-handedly took on the important project of sorting, untangling and properly inventoring all the photographs, recovering several that were thought to be lost. Her work saved untold time and expense.

On the legal and strategic side, Fred Koenigsberg, lawyer par excellence, saw to it that all the legal I's were dotted and T's were crossed with a minimum of fuss and a maximum of fine oversight and attention to what was of the essence. Richardson Love, Jr., assisted with background history and strategy in untangling us from the original publisher.

In addition, thanks and appreciation to all those who have worked diligently behind the scenes to bring this project to fruition.

It is my hope that all who read this book will also experience some of the magic of *Las artes populares* and feel the call to go see them in the market place, as Father did, experiencing the fun of collecting a few art pieces themselves, or to come to SAMA and wander in the galleries, or find where these arts are being exhibited in their own communities, or be inspired to learn more about Mexico and it's rich history, culture and the life of it's *artesanos*.

Prologue by Marion Oettinger, Jr.

The publication of this second edition of *Folk Treasures of Mexico: The Nelson A. Rockefeller Collection* is an important step toward further realization of Rockefeller's dream to highlight and celebrate the wonderful folk art of Mexico. He was enamored with Latin America, especially Mexico, where he first traveled in 1933, and art became a special way he could continue to partake in the warmth, color, exuberance and spirit of that part of the world long after his return to New York or Washington. Indeed, one of Rockefeller's last foreign visits before his death in 1979 was a whirlwind trip to Mexico with daughter, Ann, folk art specialist Annie O'Neill and others to once again explore the magic of Oaxaca during October of 1978. He was completely re-energized, and with characteristic zeal, jumped right into crowded public markets and sat down with extraordinarily talented folk artists, who at the time, had not an inkling of how profoundly their own lives and professions would be impacted by his visit and the selection of their art for his collection. To this day, snapshots of his visit still adorn the adobe walls of many of the artists in the Valley of Oaxaca. News of Rockefeller's visit quickly spread, not only throughout Mexico, but also among folk art aficionados and museums in the United States and beyond. I clearly remember my own first visit, late in 1978, to the home of the legendary Oaxaca ceramist Teodora Blanco. After I had marveled at her work and made a few small purchases, she mentioned that one of my countrymen had recently visited her, and, perhaps, I knew him. She disappeared into the backroom and emerged moments later with a glossy 8 x 10 black and white print of herself with Rockefeller holding one of her exotic figures. The photo was warmly inscribed to Doña Teodora. I explained that I only knew *of* Nelson Rockefeller.

Rockefeller's devotion to Latin America and his keen eye for very good art had made him a leader in the field and many looked to him for guidance and legitimacy. Over many decades, he and his illustrious family had left enduring marks on the cultural life of the United States, especially in major art museums such as the Metropolitan Museum of Art, the Museum of Modern Art, the Abby Aldridge Rockefeller American Folk Art Museum and other leading institutions. For Nelson Rockefeller to leave his imprimatur on a particular genre of art or the work of an individual artist, folk or fine, was not to be taken lightly—and, it never was. Rockefeller's commitment to Mexican folk art, thirty years after his death, continues to influence and shape many fields of artistic expression.

Ann Rockefeller Robert's gift of 2,500 pieces of Mexican folk art to the San Antonio Museum of Art in 1985 profoundly affected the Museum and strongly helped shape its commitment to Mexican folk art, as well as Latin American art, in general. It has attracted additional donations of art, led to increased endowment funds and provided impetus for hundreds of exhibitions, loans to other institutions, publications, internships and research projects over the past twenty-four years. Finally, this gift became a major catalyst leading to the completion, in 1998, of the Nelson A. Rockefeller Center for Latin American Art, generally considered to be the most comprehensive statement on the subject in this country.

The San Antonio Museum of Art (SAMA) is proud of its stewardship of the Rockefeller collection over more than two decades and pleased that it has grown the collection, staffed the Latin American Department with thoroughly professional personnel, published important segments of the collection and provided rich opportunities for students and fully developed scholars to work with Rockefeller materials in our possession.

ADDITIONAL ACQUISITIONS

From the very beginning, the gift of Nelson Rockefeller's collection has been a magnet for other important collections. Early on, trustees of the Robert K. Winn Collection of Mexican Folk Art agreed to donate approximately 3,000 pieces of folk and colonial art to SAMA once the Rockefeller gift had been secured. Rather than duplicate the Rockefeller collection, Winn's art greatly complemented it in content, age and materials. Furthermore, the Winn collection brought with it endowment funds to hire a full-time curator to shepherd the folk art collection through to exhibition and publication, and beyond. This endowment, in turn, has attracted additional funds through annual volunteer-run events such as Bazar Sábado, which has added over $200,000 to the endowment and paid for dozens of special lectures, small exhibitions and acquisitions.

In 1992, SAMA was given a major collection of Guatemalan indigenous textiles by Harwood and Kate Smith of Dallas that represents male and female costumes from approximately 30 villages in the highlands. Over the years, the Museum has received gifts from people around the United States who had known Rockefeller and wanted to honor their special friendship. In the late 1990s, Laurence Rockefeller, Nelson's older brother, gave the Museum important Mexican modern paintings by Diego Rivera, Jean Charlot, and others to show his appreciation for the professional manner in which SAMA had cared for his late brother's collection. Finally, knowing SAMA's serious commitment to the preservation, study, and sharing of Latin American folk art, Peter P. Cecere, an extraordinarily creative collector of nineteenth and twentieth century folk art from Spain and various parts of Latin America, gave the Museum more than 300 important works that led to a serious examination of the Spanish roots of Latin American folk art.

EXHIBITIONS AND LOANS TO OTHER MUSEUMS

Over the past twenty years, SAMA has made a strong and concerted effort to exhibit as much of the Rockefeller collection as possible. In the fall of 1986, the Museum mounted a major long-term exhibition entitled *Con Cariño: Mexican Folk Art from the Collection of the San Antonio Museum of Art*. About half of the 300 pieces on display were from the Rockefeller collection. The Museum drew extensively from the collection over the next two decades to install temporary exhibitions on Days of the Dead, votive art, folk saints, games, the Virgin of Guadalupe, Holy Week and many other subjects.

To celebrate the publication of the first edition of *Folk Treasures* in 1990, SAMA organized a special traveling exhibition of masterpieces from the Rockefeller collection that was seen in ten cities around the United States, including Los Angeles, Miami, Sacramento, Colorado Springs and other major centers of Latino population. When the tour ended two years later, several hundred thousand people had seen it—exactly what we had hoped for.

In the early 1990s, we placed 500 pieces of Latin American folk art, much of it Rockefeller material, into a national registry known as the Museum Loan Network to facilitate long-term loans to museums that have little or no art of a particular type. This program, funded by the Pew/Knight Foundations and administered by MIT, became the vehicle for a major loan of several hundred folk art pieces to the Tallahassee Museum of Art for most of a year. SAMA still participates in this creative program and looks forward to future requests.

The changing demographics of the United States over the past two decades have meant that growing Latino populations are now present in most parts of the country. Museums in many of these communities have no collections linking them to their new citizens, and SAMA has freely lent materials to these institutions. Most recently, the Public Museum in Reading, Pennsylvania, an eighteenth-century community founded by Anglo-Saxons, but now comprised of a population that is over 50 percent Latino, requested approximately 100 pieces from the Rockefeller/Winn collections, and we gladly obliged. We have lent Rockefeller materials to temporary exhibitions at Yale University, the Craft and Folk Art Museum of Los Angeles County, the museum at Florida International University, the Corcoran Museum in Washington, D.C., the Seattle Museum of Art, the Denver Art Museum, the Field Museum in Chicago, as well as other institutions, and we look forward to doing so in the future.

THE NELSON A. ROCKEFELLER CENTER FOR LATIN AMERICAN ART AND THE FUTURE

In 1991, the San Antonio Museum of Art hosted what was perhaps the greatest, most comprehensive, exhibition on Mexican art ever presented in this country: *Mexico: Splendors of Thirty Centuries*. Organized by the Metropolitan Museum of Art and the Mexican government, this ground-breaking exhibition drew more than 270,000 visitors to SAMA. The tremendous success of this exhibition and the strong Mexican heritage of the majority of San Antonio's population, spoke strongly in favor of the Museum increasing its commitment to the art of Latin America. Within a year after the close of *Splendors* the Museum set out to design and build a new wing to house and exhibit the art of Mexico and other parts of Latin America.

Exterior Windows looking into the pre-Columbian gallery of the Nelson A. Rockefeller Center (NAR) for Latin American Art.

Spanish Colonial gallery of the NAR Center for Latin American Art.

Modern/Contemporary gallery of the NAR Center for Latin American Art.

Folk Art gallery of the NAR Center for Latin American Art.

Financial support came from local and national foundations, corporations, families, the National Endowment for the Humanities, a city of San Antonio bond initiative and individuals who agreed with the Museum's mission to honor and celebrate the rich artistic heritage of Mexico, Central and South America. In recognition of his early devotion to the arts of Latin America and his love of the people of that area of the world, the Museum requested permission to name the new 30,000 square-foot center in honor of Nelson A. Rockefeller.

The Nelson A. Rockefeller Center for Latin America, that opened to the public in the fall of 1998, has four permanent galleries devoted to pre-Columbian, Spanish Colonial/Republican, Modern/Contemporary and Folk Art, as well as a small space designed for temporary exhibitions drawn mainly from the permanent collection.

At present, the third floor of the Rockefeller Center is used for storage and processing of new acquisitions. Our plans are to convert this space into a center for the study of Latin American art. It will hold our Latin American art research library and have special space for the Museum's important photographic material. In addition, the new facility will provide open storage for the majority of the Museum's smaller works in a physical environment conducive to scholarly research. We plan to have seminar rooms and research carrels for visiting scholars from around the United States and beyond. It is the Museum's hope that sufficient funds will be raised to establish endowments to operate this exciting research center and pay for the stipends of its researchers.

Finally, we are proud of the professional stewardship of the Rockefeller collection by the San Antonio Museum of Art and pleased with the ways we have leveraged this important collection so that it has grown and been shared with citizens of the United States and beyond. The new English and Spanish editions of *Folk Treasures of Mexico: The Nelson A. Rockefeller Collection* moves Rockefeller's dream quite a bit further along.

Marion Oettinger, Jr.
Curator of Latin American Art and
The Betty and Bob Kelso Director of the San Antonio Museum of Art
August 2009

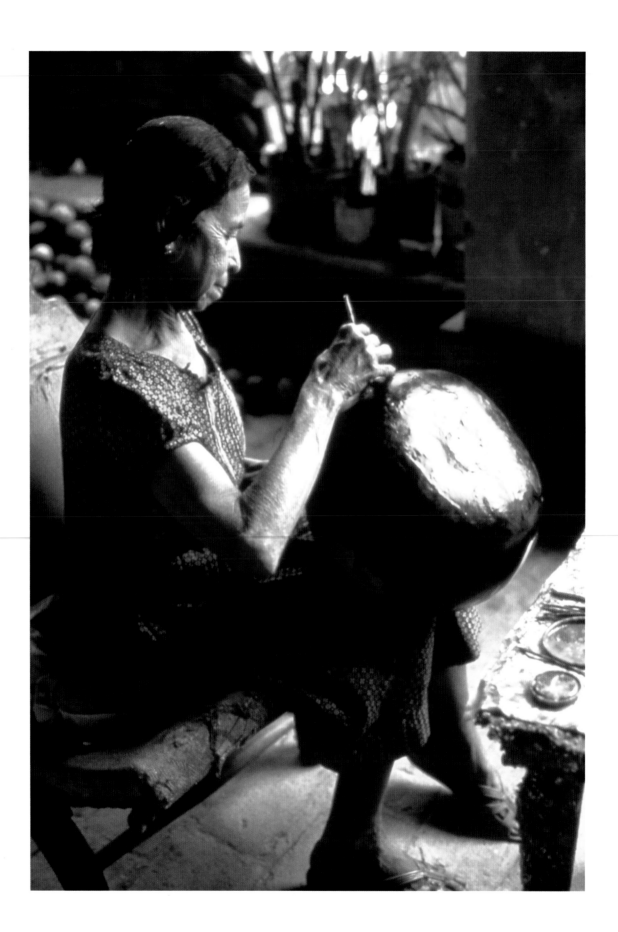

Acknowledgments

This book owes a great deal to many people. It was essentially a work of collaboration not only between author and photographers but also with others who knew Nelson Rockefeller and were able to provide valuable personal insight into his love for and commitment to Mexican folk art. Ann R. Roberts, daughter of the late Governor Rockefeller, is responsible for purchasing the collection from her father's estate and for painstakingly locating a permanent home for it, thereby assuring its preservation. She has been the catalyst for this book, and I am grateful for her vision of its necessity and importance and for her constant help, support and encouragement throughout this entire endeavor.

Annie O'Neill, artist, folk art specialist and former adviser to Nelson Rockefeller on his collection, has been a close friend and collaborator during this project. She worked closely with Rockefeller on his collection and traveled to Mexico with him and Ann R. Roberts to photograph folk artists and to make new acquisitions. She also curated the collection before it found its way to final homes in San Antonio and San Francisco. Her special sensitivity to the collection and deep respect for Nelson Rockefeller have been important to the overall success of this project.

Since an important part of understanding Mexican folk art is through visual means, it was absolutely crucial that the photographs for the book be of the highest quality. Lee Boltin, an internationally respected photographer who had collaborated with Rockefeller on two earlier art projects, began work on this material in 1978, and most of the photographs of the objects were taken by him. The rest were shot by John Dyer, from San Antonio, and Steve Tucker, of New York City. They bring to this publication not only superb understanding of photographic techniques and methods but also

Doña Rosa Real de Nieto with one of her decorative pieces, San Bartolo Coyotepec, Oaxaca, October 1978.

A lacquered gourd being carefully decorated with traditional floral motifs in Chiapa de Corzo, Chiapas, 1976.

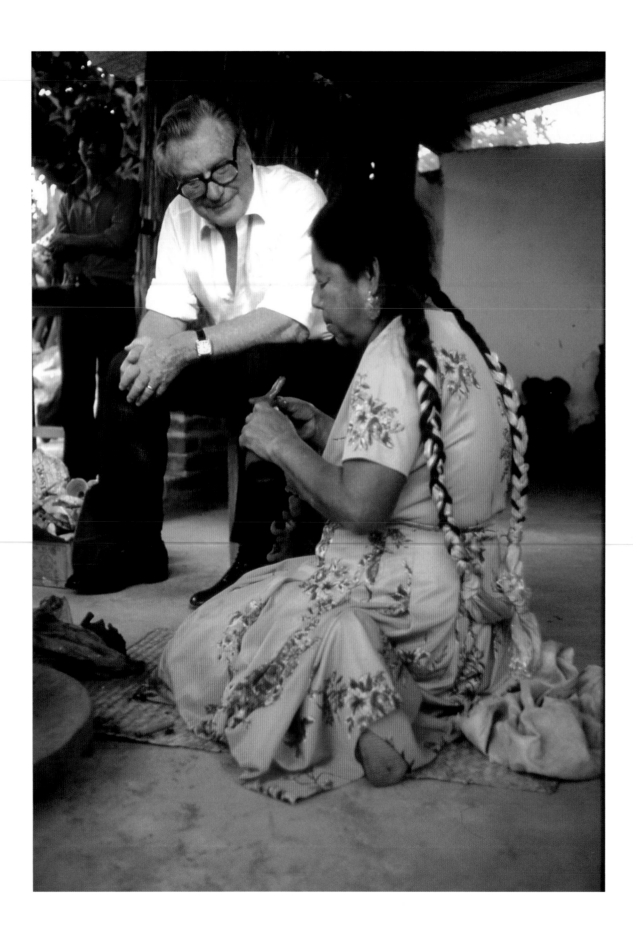

remarkable sensitivity to the objects themselves. I thank them for sharing these gifts with us.

I interviewed many people who knew Nelson Rockefeller well and who generously provided important perspectives on his great passion for art in general and his love for Mexican folk art in particular. Among those whose insights were most important to the formation of this book were Laurance Rockefeller, Mary Rockefeller, Rodman Rockefeller, Christine Roussell, Carl Fox and Susan Herter. Their views on Rockefeller's love of Mexico, her people and her art have added warmth and special understanding to our book, and I greatly appreciate the time and thoughts they shared with me. To properly understand Nelson Rockefeller's involvement in Mexican folk art requires a familiarity with the happenings of the 1930s and 1940s in Mexico that brought to light the existence of that country's popular arts. I interviewed dozens of people who collectively painted for me a vivid picture of the intellectual and artistic currents of that exciting time in Mexico that had held Rockefeller's attention so firmly. Among those whose thoughts were most helpful were Sarah d'Harnoncourt (Mrs. René), Mildred Constantine and Dr. Merle Wachter.

Dr. Joseph Ernst, director emeritus of the Rockefeller Archive Center in North Tarrytown, New York, generously gave of his time, knowledge and energy to guide me through myriad boxes of documents, and his kind assistance is greatly appreciated. Claire Collier, also of the center, graciously assisted me in locating valuable photographs in the archives, some of which are included in this book.

I also acknowledge the help of Mary Kreske and Kendall Lutkins, of the Rockefeller offices in New York City, who kindly assisted me in locating other important relevant material that had not yet found its way to the permanent family archives.

Few manuscripts make it into print without the help of good editors, and I was lucky to have several people who read and commented on mine. John Mahey, former director of the San Antonio Museum of Art, and John Olbrecht carefully read my manuscript and made valuable comments on content and style. Patty Spencer, Gretchen Schumacher and Didi Cowley

Rockefeller talking with Teodora Blanco, Santa María Atzompa, Oaxaca, October 1978.

also helped with the manuscript preparation, and I thank them for their assistance. Baker Duncan and Dr. Ronald Calgaard of Trinity University in San Antonio generously arranged an office for me to escape the clutter and clatter of my normal museum work space, and I thank them for their kind hospitality. I worked closely with several key people at Abrams on the editing and production phases of this book. Margaret Rennolds, Abrams' project director for this publication, did an excellent job of sorting out inconsistencies and duplications in both form and content. She shepherded the manuscript through its many steps toward production, and I thank her for her skillful labors. Dana Sloan, who designed the book, showed that she has not only a keen eye for design but also a strong sensitivity for the text and photographs.

Finally, I thank my wife, Jill, for abiding the great amount of time I had to spend away from home and for her love and support during this entire project.

Marion Oettinger, Jr.
Curator of Folk Art and Latin American Art,
San Antonio Museum of Art,
San Antonio, Texas

n addition to joining with my own heartfelt thanks in acknowledging the many people recognized by Marion Oettinger, Jr., I would like to make a few acknowledgments of my own.

This book had a firm base in the splendid photographs taken by Lee Boltin, which made all the difference in putting it together after Father's death. The delight Father had in Lee's company and their banter as they worked was a pleasure to see and reflected the spirit of both men. Annie O'Neill has been a wonderful friend and collaborator throughout this entire process. From the initial search for a home for the collection, to the selection of photographs, the writing of the commentaries on the plates and almost every other phase of the book, she has lent her untiring support and considerable skills. Before the collection was released to its final homes, the inventory was done meticulously by David Fawcett; he also organized the packing and shipping of the fragile objects with tender care and attention to every detail.

The staff, trustees and friends of both the San Antonio Museum of Art (SAMA) and the Mexican Museum (MM), in San Francisco, were wonderfully efficient and attentive to the collection during the transition. I am particularly grateful to John Mahey, the former director of the SAMA, and David de la Torre, the former director of the MM, for their guidance and the enjoyment of working with them. I am most appreciative of the generosity of the SAMA in allowing Marion Oettinger to take a leave of absence in order to research and write the text for this book. His fine work as an anthropologist, a researcher and a writer speaks for itself in the quality of his text, and it has also been a real pleasure to work with him. His unflagging enthusiasm for this project and his devotion to Mexican folk art inform every part of his contribution. Avon Neal's willingness to take time out from his own folk art work to write the introduction is very much appreciated and brings an important dimension to the book as well.

In addition to the editors already mentioned, my thanks go to Jon Swan for his substantial assistance with the organization of the text. Richard Parsons' legal skills and clearheadedness were essential in untangling the book from past commitments, and he gave willingly of his time.

Finally, my thanks go to my family for encouraging me to take on this project and see it through to completion. My uncle Laurance never waived in his support of me and his belief in this book. He and Father's widow, Happy Rockefeller, made it possible for me to acquire the collection and the rights to the book. My children and my husband T. George Harris were unquestioning in their loving support and enthusiasm.

—*Ann Rockefeller Roberts*

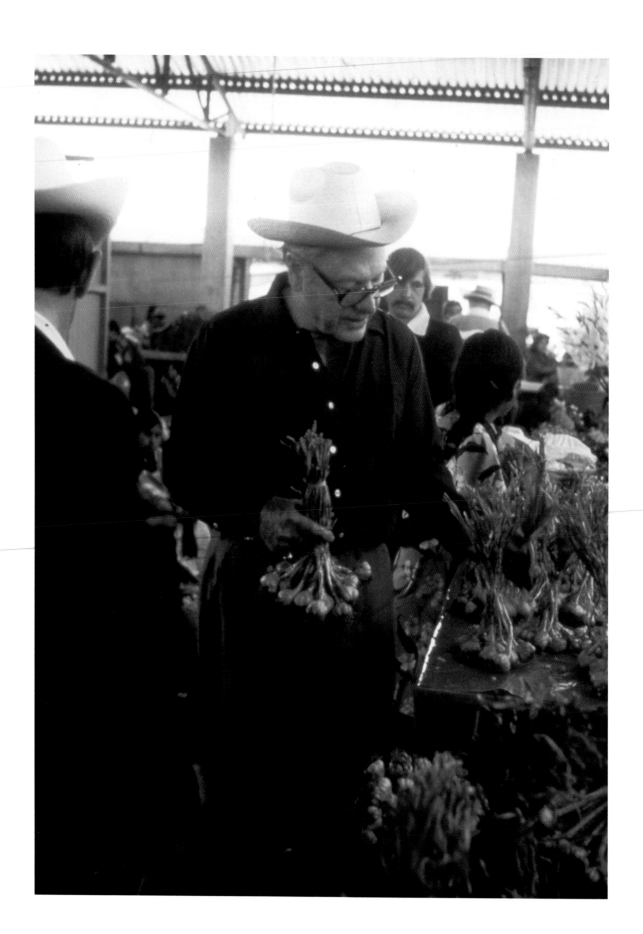

Foreword by Nelson A. Rockefeller

October/November 1978

s I start to write these words for the introduction of this book on "Arte Popular de México," I'm flying across the Gulf of Mexico, on my way to Oaxaca to participate in the celebrations of the Día de los Muertos—the Day of the Dead. In Mexico, and especially in Oaxaca, this is a day of special significance in the Indian folklore of the country. It is celebrated by an outpouring of the entire community following weeks of preparation by local craftsmen who create the original, colorful and exotic figures, decorations, costumes and carvings that become an integral part of the celebration. The Day of the Dead, as no other festival in Mexico, brings forth joyously the traditions of past centuries. It reveals in heightened form the unique qualities of the Mexican people, qualities that combine an inherent sense of human dignity with sensitivity and gentleness; great imagination and fantastic ability with love of family and pride in the country's rich and varied cultural heritage.

To one who loves Mexico and the Mexican people and profoundly admires the breathtaking evidences of their twenty centuries of artistic creations, this great festival day has to be one of the most thrilling experiences of one's life. The people are living and celebrating the quintessence of their heritage in a setting of unparalleled beauty—the great temples of Monte Albán reflecting the dignity and glory of the Zapotec civilization, which flourished in the sixth century B.C. and the monumental Spanish colonial cathedrals, the most beautiful of which in Oaxaca is Santo Domingo, built in the sixteenth century for the Spanish conquistadors with exquisite skill by the Indian artisans of the conquered Aztec empire.

In Oaxaca one sees the drama of this endless flow of creativity still pulsating with the vitality of a great people.

Rockefeller buying garlic in the Ocotlán market, Ocotlán de Morelos, Oaxaca, October 1978.

Mexican popular art is the outgrowth of this great tradition that, throughout the centuries, has been an integral part of various aspects of the daily lives of the people. It comprises objects made for utilitarian purposes, as religious symbols and for festivals and celebrations of all kinds—but always expressing the creativity and imagination of the individual artists-craftsmen who fashioned them.

It was just forty-five years ago, in 1933, that I first went to Mexico and discovered the beauty and excitement of this unique land. By good fortune, my wife and I had planned an extensive visit to widely varied regions of the country with their distinct histories and fascinating characteristics.

We were fortunate in the friends we made—Diego Rivera, Miguel and Rosa Covarrubias, Fred Davis, Roberto Montenegro and Frances Flynn Paine—for it was through their eyes and thanks to their great kindness that we were privileged to see and begin to appreciate the four great epic phases of Mexico's cultural history: the monumental works of the pre-Columbian civilizations, the richness of the colonial period, the unending flow of indigenous popular art and the tremendous vitality of the modern art movement.

But perhaps the most exciting part of that trip was the time we spent in the small cities, villages and rural areas with Frances Flynn Paine. Frances had devoted her life to studying the popular arts of the Mexican people. Her knowledge of the art and of the artists throughout the country was en-cyclopedic. Her love of their works was matched by the affection and respect each artist-craftsman felt for her.

It was a privilege to travel with her from marketplace to marketplace, where the colorful displays—and beautiful fascinating objects—left one breathless. My fascination and enthusiasm resulted in endless purchases of an infinite variety of pottery, wood carvings, sarapes and handwoven rugs, ranging in price from a few cents to a few dollars. However, invariably there were one or two craftsmen in each area whose work was outstanding and to whose homes we were taken by Frances. There we came to know the gentle warmth and hospitality so typical of the Mexican people and experience the thrill of watching creation in its simplest and most genuine form. Thanks to

Frances' knowledge and love of the people and their art, we gained unique insight into Mexican popular art.

I have never stopped collecting in this field since. Now, forty-five years after that first visit, I am on my way back to Oaxaca for a final visit before completing this book on one of the most exciting and colorful phases in the rich cultural history of Mexico. With me in the airplane are my daughter Ann R. Roberts and Lee Boltin, the photographer for the book.

Teodora Blanco with Rockefeller's daughter Ann R. Roberts, Santa María Atzompa, Oaxaca, October 1978.

Annie O'Neill and Carl Fox were at the airport to meet us, having made all the arrangements for the ensuing day's visits.

The extraordinary good fortune was that some of the greatest original artists and potters were still creating with the same vigor, insights and sensitivities: Teodora Blanco, Doña Rosa and members of the Aguilar family.

We went, that first afternoon, directly to Teodora Blanco's house in a small village outside of Oaxaca. She was there with her large family, including children and relatives, all living in a courtyard with lovely trees, flowers, old buildings, chickens, goats and a little pig tied with a string to an old broken-down truck. The little pig kept up a shrill squeal until, about halfway through our visit, someone finally fed it. Teodora worked on the veranda of the house, which also served as a storage place for her pottery figures. The kiln was in the courtyard, just in front.

Our arrival was like a reunion full of warmth and enthusiasm. After the initial greetings and *abrazos*, Teodora showed us her latest, almost monumental, figures, which were more elaborately decorated than her earlier work. Later, as we watched her sculpt as she swiftly modeled an allegorical horned figure holding a child in each arm, describing what she was doing as she worked, it was easy to understand the evolution in her work. She is a person of such an active mind, so feeling and creative, that one thought leads to another and each is expressed in sculptural form through some additions to or elaboration of the piece in hand—with lightning speed and sensitivity.

The result is that her compositions increasingly resemble the paintings of her environs in both their imagination and their bizarre compositions.

Annie O'Neill visiting the home of Doña Rosa during the October 1978 trip to Mexico.

Ceramic artist Teodora Blanco, of
Santa María Atzompa, surrounded
by her pieces, reveals her stylistic
facility and typical use of abundant
surface decoration, October 1978.

We spent two fascinating hours with Teodora, talking with her and selecting objects for purchase. Although they ranged in price from a few cents to less than a hundred dollars for her largest monumental piece, aesthetically they represented a subtle sophistication possessed by but few of the finest contemporary artists. Already we felt more than rewarded for the two-thousand-mile trip.

After leaving Teodora, we drove farther out into the country to a larger village with a large plaza shaded by majestic old trees. This was Ocotlán. The plaza was carpeted with the most colorful pottery, basketwork, raffia weaving and wooden furniture. Woolen handwoven sarapes and blankets hung on ropes strung between trees. The entire area was alive with Indians, the men wearing big hats, coming and going, picking their way through the crowds, buying and selling, while the women sat quietly, weaving raffia, embroidering, feeding their babies and enjoying the hustle and bustle of this important weekly social event.

We wove our way through the fabulous variety of objects, one more fascinating than the next, watching potters paint their wares, and all the time trying to spot the unusual and especially beautiful creations. We bought objects here and there, and as we came back to where the great displays of pottery were spread out, Annie O'Neill presented me with a large, beautifully decorated dish that she had had the artist inscribe: *"Al gobernador, un recuerdo de Ocotlán"* ("to the governor, a souvenir of Ocotlán"), which was typical of her thoughtful sensitivity and love of Mexican popular art.

Chili and vegetable vendors, Ocotlán de Morelos, Oaxaca, October 1978.

From Ocotlán we drove, at sunset, up the mountain to the monumental Zapotec temples, from which one looks out over the whole valley. There the ancestors of the Oaxaca Indians of today flourished more than 2,500 years ago. The dignity and cultural vitality of the ancestors live on in a never-ending flow of creativity and in the people's respect for the honor of the individual.

The events of that first day brought back vivid memories of the very similar days we had spent with Frances Flynn Paine forty-five years before.

I remember especially two experiences—one, a visit to the last of the great sarape weavers, an elderly Indian woman whose weaving was so fine

Pottery vendor at the Friday market, Ocotlán de Morelos, Oaxaca, October 1978.

Woman arranging lemons at the Friday market, Ocotlán de Morelos, Oaxaca, October 1978.

that no one of the younger generation had the patience to develop the skills required to carry it on. I was so excited by her wonderful work that I bought virtually her entire collection. Although I have continued to collect hand-woven sarapes and blankets ever since, I have never found anything to compare with the work of that beautiful and gentle little lady who was so pleased by the joy we derived from her works.

The other experience that stands out in my memory from that first visit to Mexico was my encounter with the outstanding Indian sculptor Mardonio Magaña, in Mexico City. We first saw one of his works in a square near the San Angel Inn, at which we were staying, in a Mexico City suburb. This piece of sculpture evidenced such sensitivity and humanity, as well as artistic quality, that I asked Mrs. Paine if she could make arrangements for a visit to his studio.

Mardonio Magaña was as beautiful and gentle as his sculpture. Without hesitation, I bought two of his stone pieces and two wood carvings, each of which manifested the same deep love and sensitive human understanding of the Mexican campesino that I had found in his larger piece in the square.

There was an immediate bond of sympathy between us, and out of this grew a warm friendship. Magaña asked if we would like to visit the school he had started to teach children to sculpt. We said we would be delighted, and the following day we went with him to the school. It was an overwhelming experience—a few dozen children in their teens working on a wide variety of stones, carving wood or casting in metal. The quality of their work, inspired by this extraordinary man, was unbelievably good.

I couldn't help thinking of the enormous reserves of talent that existed among the Indian people of this great country—talent that the rulers and high priests of the pre-Columbian emperors had so effectively mobilized and that the Spanish conquistadors and the clergy of the Spanish Church had again called upon to create one of the richest and most beautiful colonial periods in history.

There, in Mardonio Magaña's studio, five hundred years after the first Spanish architect-builders had retrained Indian artisans, those same talents were being awakened and redirected into modern forms of expression. It was a moving experience to see these young artists so absorbed in their work. We watched in wonder at the way Magaña—through his example and his love—inspired them to create in a totally natural and unselfconscious manner.

I asked with some hesitation whether it might be possible to purchase a few pieces. Magaña was thrilled and said the children would be delighted because we were the first people to have visited the school and none of the children's work had ever been sold. I ended up buying twenty-two pieces for a total of $220. No purchase has given me more lasting pleasure.

Since my first visit to Mexico in the 1930s, I have sensed something strong, imaginative and beautiful about her popular arts, and I have collected it and lived with it in my house ever since.

Preface by Ann Rockefeller Roberts

This book represents the final stage of a ten-year odyssey that began in 1979, shortly after the death of my father, Nelson Aldrich Rockefeller.

It all started with a phone call from him on a Wednesday afternoon in October of 1978. Without preamble and in his exuberant way, he asked if I would like to go to Mexico on Friday for the weekend. Somehow it was clear to me that there might not be another chance like this, so, canceling my own plans, I flew off with my father. It was an amazing weekend, both a mad buying spree and a revisiting of old times and old places. It turned out to be the last trip of this kind he was to make. He died just three months later.

As a result of the trip, I became fully aware for the first time of the extent of Father's Mexican folk art collection and its priceless quality. Even though part of it was exhibited in 1968 at the Museum of Primitive Art in New York, which he founded, most of the collection had been in storage for years, and no one in his family had ever seen it all. Father had unpacked the entire collection early in 1978 in order to have it photographed for this book. It was arrayed on shelf after shelf in a large storage area. His pleasure at seeing it again let loose a flood of stories about his love of folk art and his years of deep involvement in Latin America. It turned out there were nearly 3,000 pieces, many of them no longer being made or extremely rare.

After his death, it became apparent that no one knew exactly what to do with all these thousands of pieces of folk art created by village artists who were better understood by travelers than by museum critics. The works were in danger of being auctioned off or divided up among family members.

Neither option made sense to me. I felt the collection should be preserved and put in a place where both Anglo-Americans and people of Latin

A potter loading his below-ground kiln in Amozoc, Puebla, October 1978.

descent could see it. Only in that way could the visions that my father had devoted many years working toward in the early part of his career be realized.

The Rockefeller collection is now securely and happily established in not one, but two excellent museums. The major portion is at the San Antonio Museum of Art, the premier art museum in San Antonio, Texas. The other part of the collection is housed at the Mexican Museum in San Francisco, one of the only American museums founded by a Mexican-American artist. In these places, North Americans can see the richness of Mexican culture through her folk arts, and Mexican Americans can see their own abundant Spanish and Indian folk heritage fully honored—a solution that reflects my father's respect for Latin culture and his desire for it to be represented in the United States.

Publishing this book completes a journey for me as well—the search for a deeper understanding of my father's early involvement with Mexican folk art. This is his book. It honors his unwavering love of Mexican folk art, the Mexican people and the Mexican culture. He believed in the beauty and artistic power of these pieces, in their lasting value and in the skill of their creators. He enjoyed many other forms of folk art—American, African, Native American, Indian and Southeast Asian. However, Mexican folk art was a passion that endured throughout his life, resurfacing whenever there was an opening for him in time or space.

The Mexican people and their art connected Father with a deep part of himself. Their exuberance, their close relation to the earth's natural processes and their sense of the sacredness of the routines of their daily lives were in tune with Father's own inner processes. His naturally extroverted nature blossomed when surrounded by their enthusiasm. I remember, as a child, watching with delight and fascination as father greeted his Mexican friends with a hearty *abrazo*, a natural Latin greeting that would have been impossible among his acquaintances in New York. I think that his love of the Mexican marketplace had as much to do with the openness and vitality of the life there as with the chance to find new treasures.

These folk artists that Father was drawn to were part of a culture in which the ordinary events of daily life were celebrated: birth, infancy, adolescence, courtship, marriage, old age and death. An enormous amount of creative energy was showered onto the special objects that manifested the deeper meaning of these events. He and I came from a culture where the celebrations of life's passages were carefully controlled and made so tidy, that they were often not fully experienced. Through his folk art collection, Father could savor the Latin joy in life even when he could not be there among the artisans.

This love and understanding of the importance of the ordinary to the essential vitality of life is perhaps the most treasured of the many things I learned from my father. He knew instinctively that the mundane things made to carry out everyday acts—the containers we put things in, the clothing we wear, the religious objects we pray with, the toys we give our children—are all valuable and worthy of the greatest creative expression.

He could also see that it is the nature of the cycles of life to repeat themselves and that folk artists recreate each new birth, life or death through their art. In this way, the folk arts allow us to renew our own experience and understand the uniqueness of each human passage.

So, reader, in these pages, come to the marketplace with the exuberant collector, my father, who taught me the beauty of the myriad colorful tools of Mexican daily living and who loved the rich flavors of Mexican life.

The human hand, always felt in Mexican folk art, meant a lot to Rockefeller. In this photograph we see the hands of Elena Carillo Hernández at work on a *tabla*, pressing yarn into beeswax, Mexico City, October 1978.

Introduction by Avon Neal

Mexico holds a unique place in the context of modern folk art. Its artisans produce some of the world's most exciting and creative examples of art for the common man. Using whatever materials are found at hand, both organic and inorganic, they fashion a fantastic array of utilitarian and decorative objects ranging from simple toys to highly elaborate ceremonial and religious art. While most of these creations are regional, even local, in concept and design, they have in common a distinctly Mexican character that gives them a supreme sense of national identity. Many of these objects are pre-Hispanic in origin and can be traced by a continuous line through Spanish colonial times to the present day.

Elena Carillo Hernández, from Las Pilas, Santa Catarina, Nayarit, working on a large yarn painting (*tabla*) in Mexico City, October 1978.

Since the early twentieth century, when a widespread cultural awakening inspired a lively interest in things folkloric, Mexico's popular arts have flourished, more or less, in accordance to demand. As tourism increased that demand, local craftsmen labored to meet it. The recent advent of museum shops and specialty stores dealing in ethnic arts is mainly responsible for introducing the best—and, often, the worst—of Mexican folk art to the general public and for elevating it to the exalted position it enjoys today. Well-informed buyers tirelessly scour the countryside searching out hitherto-undiscovered yet talented artists while a whole new generation of discriminating collectors is helping to keep the tradition alive. It is estimated that one person in every six of Mexico's population is involved, either full- or part-time, in the manufacture and sale of "popular art."

After the tragic upheaval of the 1910 revolution—"the wind that swept Mexico"—a wave of confidence pervaded all levels of Mexican society, and during the 1920s a bold new nationalism took hold of the land. Artists and intellectuals began to explore their country's Indian heritage, discovering untapped sources of inspiration for their creative endeavors. A handful of connoisseurs and prominent painters, already fascinated by pre-Columbian artifacts, began collecting examples of the everyday art objects that were commonplace in markets. Some of these, they were quick to proclaim, bore an uncanny resemblance to the antique pieces they admired and assiduously collected. They were convinced that these contemporary pieces—carved, molded, woven, painted; some grotesquely beautiful, others inventively decorated utilitarian objects—represented a truly indigenous art expression that sprang from the hearts of their people. They saw in these objects a connection to Mexico's archaeological past, a national heritage, to be appreciated and preserved, something to be championed in the wider world of art.

During the 1930s and 1940s, interest in Mexican folk culture increased by leaps and bounds. Writings on the subject began to appear in books and popular journals. It was not long before exhibitions were being mounted at home and abroad. Viewers liked what they saw and promptly fell into step with the inquisitive surge toward south-of-the-border civilizations that had lately occupied intellectually curious travelers. Tourism from across the northern border was developing rapidly, helping to stimulate arts and crafts production. Merchandising began in earnest, with a number of well-stocked shops such as Cervantes, Victor's Artes Populares Mexicanos and the colorful but touristy Sanborn's House of Tiles in Mexico City, supplying eager buyers with a wide variety of handcrafted objects. Souvenir hunters and serious collectors vied with one another in open-air markets as haphazard accumulations were gradually organized into rudimentary private collections. It was a heady excursion into unexplored territory for those involved with collecting indigenous arts and crafts.

Nelson Rockefeller was in this vanguard of Mexican folk art aficionados. His collecting activities had already brought him into the company of several distinguished Mexican painters, who encouraged and advised him on matters of Latin American art. These were eminent artists such as Miguel Covarrubias, Diego Rivera, Gerardo Murillo (better known as Dr. Atl), Roberto Montenegro and others who were engaged in revealing the folkloric mysteries of their country's past. As he listened to them extolling the artistic merits of the charming handcrafted objects they were discovering almost daily in local marketplaces, Rockefeller was quick to realize the validity of this art form. It wasn't long before he found himself sharing their passion for what was then most frequently referred to as *artes populares*. He soon succumbed to temptation and started a random gathering of representative pieces on his own. From that time forward, he never stopped.

For Rockefeller, collecting was a labor of love. Luckily, he was not hampered by the conservative academic fetters that so often restrict curators. He simply purchased whatever struck his fancy. It is to his credit and our good fortune that he had the vision and energy to pursue this newfound interest—and, one might add, the means, although money was hardly a factor, since the cost of the carvings, paintings, weavings and other hand-crafted items that so excited those early connoisseurs was reckoned in favorably exchanged pesos and sometimes even in centavos. Although he limited himself to buying only those objects that pleased him, Rockefeller soon accumulated a richly diversified assortment of wonderful folk art pieces, among them some of the finest examples from that fertile period of the 1920s, 1930s and 1940s. It is a tribute to the man that his efforts resulted in such an extensive and spectacularly varied collection.

Even before his duties as coordinator of the Office of Inter-American Affairs took him officially to Latin America, Rockefeller had acquired an intimate firsthand knowledge of Mexican folk artists and the things they produced. Whenever and wherever he could, he sought out the work of the most skilled and imaginative artisans to augment his growing collection. He visited these people in their humble dwellings, chatted with them in their own language, shared their food and closely observed how they worked. His open, easy manner fit perfectly with their Latin nature.

The search for superior examples of folk arts and crafts was exhilarating. Dedicated collectors never knew what they might come upon in the next marketplace. One thing was certain: beautiful handwrought art objects were coming to light every day.

A few artisans achieved reputations as particularly talented craftsmen. They often signed their work, and as competition grew among collectors, they were able to command higher prices for the things they produced. Signing handcrafted items was mostly a matter of personal pride. Once a proper evaluation of folk art was initiated, however, signatures proved important to scholars as a means of facilitating identification and helping to establish a particular piece's provenance. As is the case with most folk-produced art, the large majority of craftsmen remained anonymous. Nonetheless, from that great body of artisans issued a steady flow of vigorous folk art, some pieces every bit as beautiful and skillfully wrought as any of those bearing prestigious signatures. Aesthetic criteria were already being formulated.

In some areas, the makers of folk art seem determined to outdo themselves. An illustrative example involves the Indian's preoccupation with death. In a three-day festival ending on the second of November, Mexico celebrates its traditional Day of the Dead, the nation's most important Indian fiesta. It is famous for the multitudinous ways in which death is alternately mocked and romanticized by young and old alike. This ritual outpouring has contributed an entire genre of festive figures to the folk art repertory. The best are those made in the shape of skulls and skeletons posed in comic, everyday attitudes. Transcending any sense of morbidity, these reminders of man's foibles and mortality often find inspiration in the engravings of Mexico's turn-of-the-century satiric artist José Guadalupe Posada. In turn this great innovator had himself been influenced by graphic and sculptural interpretations of death personified in the folkloric tradition of an ancient cultural background. Workaday artisans—toy-makers, folk painters, clay modelers, woodcarvers, indeed, the whole community of craftspeople—happily devote themselves to this macabre theme. Collectors who prowl village marketplaces just prior to the Day of the Dead can still find folk art treasures strikingly similar to those that so intrigued Rockefeller and his fellow devotees half a century ago.

No dyed-in-the-wool collector will deny that half the fun of collecting is in the chase. For Mexican folk art enthusiasts that chase inevitably leads to the marketplace, whether it be in an urban center or in an isolated mountain village where Indian craftsmen gather on designated days to sell their wares.

Some of the best specialized collections (such as those of Nativity tableaux, wooden animals or lacquerware trays and boxes) have been assembled by hardy souls willing to brave intolerable weather conditions, exasperating transportation problems and claustrophobia-inducing crowds.

The Mexican market system has been a thriving enterprise for centuries. Examples of certain handicrafts bartered there in pre-Hispanic times can still be found today. Although modernization has sharply modified some of the articles offered for sale, a zealous collector will usually come away with folk art treasures fashioned along traditional lines—pottery in its myriad forms, woven textiles, painted toys, carved gourds, plain or decorated wooden masks or various utensils for use in field and home.

As in ancient times, today's trading centers swarm with Indians—and, more likely than not, insatiable collectors can be spotted in the crowds. Anyone who has ever visited a village market and been caught up in its stream of bustling humanity will agree that it is an unforgettable experience. Market days are festive occasions and the marketplace itself is a scene of pure exuberance. The exotic sights and riotous colors, the cacophony of sound, and the pungent and aromatic smells blend together to create a fantastic carnival atmosphere. What to an outsider appears to be utter chaos is in reality a controlled exchange of material goods. Despite visible evidence of modern encroachments, the market-day pattern remains essentially unchanged. It is almost a ritualistic performance.

Traditional market days are still observed. Many existed as highlights on the social calendar during Aztec, Toltec and Mayan times, and were described in detail by Cortez and chroniclers of the conquest. The same kinds of handcrafted products appear in their assigned places. Members of the same families who once counted Rockefeller and his artist friends as customers continue to pursue their respective crafts and to work as regular vendors. Just as they have done from time immemorial, backcountry Indians trek for days through desert wastes or along mountainous trails, carrying heavy loads of pottery and countless other wares. Trucks and buses bring itinerant peddlers from the capital or nearby towns with factory-manufactured goods. The raucous cries of hawkers and vendors compete with the chime of cathedral bells and the blare of jukebox music from cantinas, with the honking of horns and the guttural growl of overloaded buses trying to make their way through milling crowds.

Mexico's complex network of roads and highways, with connections extending from the capital to hundreds of outlying Indian communities, has facilitated a modern-day cultural diffusion in the distribution of arts and crafts. First-, second- and third-class buses ply the highways at all hours. Since fares are cheap, vendors often travel long distances to sell their wares, thereby perpetuating the classic textbook exchange of goods and ideas. During holidays and special celebrations, buyers join sellers to ride bus lines with such eye-catching and deceptively speed-suggestive names as "Galgos" (Greyhounds), "Estrella Blanca" (White Star) and "Flecha Roja" (Red Arrow) as they follow what are often the same routes traversed by their ancestors to traditional markets in some of the country's remotest villages.

Nelson Rockefeller loved marketplaces. Seeking and finding in exotic surroundings appealed to his spirit of adventure. Much of his Mexican folk art collection is the result of on-the-spot selections made in regional market centers. He had a keen eye for things beautiful and unusual, and he possessed, as well, the inveterate collector's joy of discovery and acquisition. His idea of great fun was to stroll through a busy marketplace, mingling with the colorful crowds that thronged cobbled streets and village plazas. He reveled in sampling local foods, trying out his Spanish, pausing at vendors' stalls and striking up conversations with them. He scrutinized their wares before making a selection. Once satisfied with an object, he made his purchase and hurried on to the next possibility. He thoroughly enjoyed these interchanges and delighted in the pieces he brought home.

The Mexico of Rockefeller's era is fondly remembered as a time when tourists could still count on one hand the traffic lights in downtown Mexico City; when ox carts and burros were common sights along the capital's broad avenues and dusty side streets; when the ubiquitous taxicabs cruised at curbside with beeping horns to solicit fares; when organ-grinders and itinerant photographers pursued their precarious livelihoods in the spacious grounds of Alameda Park; when *cargadores*, those human beasts of burden, could be seen straining against sweaty tumplines as they shuffled along under inhumanly heavy loads; when sidewalks were uncrowded and there were no skyscrapers to block the sun; when noise levels were tolerable and the city's air was unpolluted; when the residential *colonias* were still distinctly separate; when street vendors' cries broke each morning's silence; when village Indians, lately come to town, could still be recognized by their unique costumes; when Mexico City, with all its cultural ebullience and colonial grandeur, was the nation's great gathering place. That was the metropolis that charmed travelers and stimulated collectors to seek out and define the nation's essence in its popular arts and crafts.

Over the years, including a final buying trip to his old haunts in Mexico shortly before his death, Rockefeller amassed more than three thousand representative examples of Mexican folk art, some of them among the best available from that fruitful early period. As with all great collections, this one reflects a unique personal vision, as well as its creator's deep commitment to an indigenous art. The Nelson A. Rockefeller Mexican folk art collection represents a marvelous achievement by a very remarkable man.

Avon Neal
North Brookfield, Massachusetts

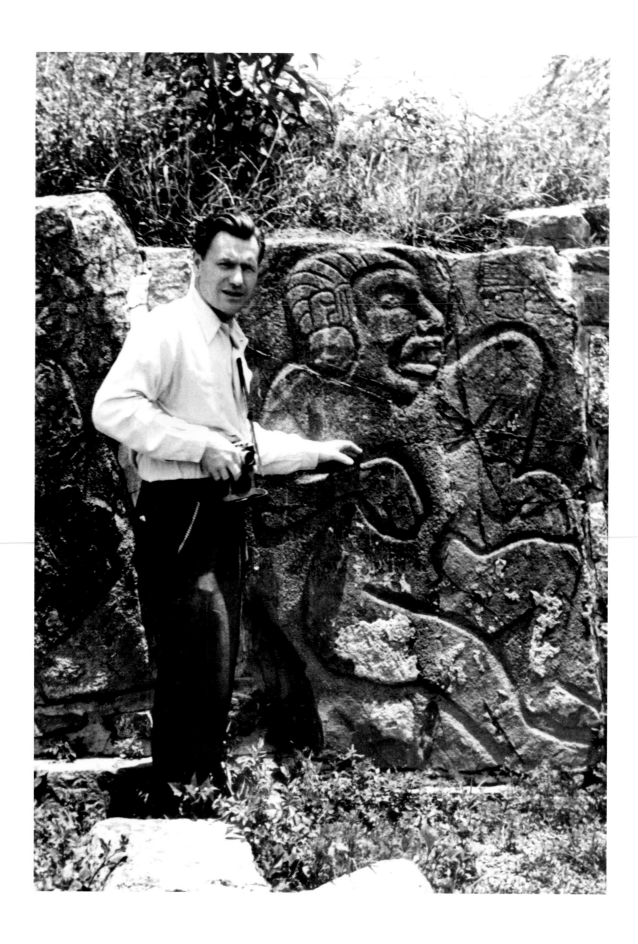

Rockefeller the Collector

By now I was rapidly gaining a more catholic understanding of the word "art." I saw "art" as widely varying expressions of individuals—individuals from all parts of the world and from all ages, with strong feelings and great creative capacities to express those feelings. No longer was my appreciation confined to classical forms of art as taught in our schools and shown in our great universities.

—Nelson A. Rockefeller[1]

n the spring of 1969 the New York art world hummed with excitement over the simultaneous openings of three important exhibitions. At the Metropolitan Museum of Art, an exhibition of one thousand pieces of primitive art from Oceania, Africa and the Americas left visitors dazzled by the intrinsic power and dramatic scale of these long-overlooked objects. Thirty blocks away, at the Museum of Modern Art, the public was treated to a remarkably comprehensive survey of modern art: more than two hundred paintings and sculptures by Cubists, Futurists, Dadaists and Abstract Expressionists. And, just around the corner, at the Museum of Primitive Art, more than seven hundred pieces of Mexican folk art reminded the public of Mexico's rich cultural heritage. These three exhibitions represented the best of the creative work of people from all over the world, much of which had been previously dismissed as unimportant by the Western art establishment.

Astonishingly, all three exhibitions were drawn from the collections of one man, Nelson A. Rockefeller, then governor of New York, later vice president of the United States. The exhibitions provided a close look at the collections of a man who had been given every opportunity to be at the very center of fashionable collecting but who had, instead, chosen to go his own way. While most of his peers were collecting the long-accepted works of the

Rockefeller at Monte Albán in 1948.

▲▲1

Old Masters and the Impressionists, and European and Oriental porcelains, Rockefeller enthusiastically embraced the aesthetic values and artistic creativity of African tribesmen, Mexican peasants and New Guinean hunters, as well as relatively unknown contemporary painters and sculptors from the United States and abroad. At the time of his death, in 1979, Rockefeller's entire personal collection contained well over sixteen thousand objects and was recognized internationally for its superb quality and extraordinary range of vision. His activities in the world of art went far beyond mere collecting to demonstrate a strong advocacy of the art that he loved best and an unflagging support both for individual artists and for the public institutions involved in the exhibition and preservation of their work.

Nelson Rockefeller's fascination with and dedication to art in general, and folk and primitive art in particular, were the result of a number of factors. Family, environment and schooling all contributed to opening up the artistic paths he would pursue in later years.

Being born into one of America's wealthiest families could have isolated Rockefeller in the rarified circles of the rich and famous. Owing to the concerted efforts of his parents, it did not. Instead of sending him to the elite, conservative private schools in the Northeast, his parents enrolled him in New York's Lincoln School, where more attention was given to the study of modern culture and social science than to the classics. From its beginning, Lincoln School provided scholarships for poor and minority students, and so, early on, Nelson was able, and encouraged, to mix with a wide cross section of people.

At the age of eighteen, he entered Dartmouth. During his four years there, his interest in art developed in a variety of ways. He became editor-in-chief of the *Dartmouth Pictorial*, a photographic magazine recording campus life (he took many of the photographs himself). He also became editor of *The Five Lively Arts*, a short-lived journal that featured the works of poets, musicians and painters. In his senior year he was elected president of The Arts, a student club that brought to Dartmouth such distinguished speakers as Carl Sandburg, Edna St. Vincent Millay and Thornton Wilder, as well as a number of gifted painters. During this year, too, he became interested in

American country furniture and folk art, enthusiastically combing the countryside around Hanover, New Hampshire, until he had assembled an impressive collection of Americana. Much of this collection would later be used to furnish Hawes House, his residence on the family's Pocantico Hills estate in Tarrytown, New York.

Although he majored in economics at Dartmouth, Nelson was continually torn between that "logical choice" and another one in which he was becoming passionately involved: art. This conflict would remain with him for the rest of his life and become at times a source of great frustration. Throughout his years at Dartmouth he managed to slip into his schedule a course or two in art. In his senior year, he pursued the study of art, architecture and landscape architecture. Characteristically, he attacked these subjects with great zeal. His energetic approach to life and art is clearly seen in a letter to his parents in 1930, just months before graduation:

> *Yesterday, I spent the most interesting kind of day possible. In the morning, I went to the Boston Art Museum and spent several hours in the American wing. Then I visited the Egyptian and Greek wings for an hour or so. Before lunch, I stopped at the Boston Library to see the Sargent paintings. In the afternoon, I went out to Cambridge and we made a thorough tour of the Fogg Museum. It was great. Then we stopped in at the Harvard Library to look it over and see Sargent's two murals. And finally we went to visit the exhibition of Modern Mexican painters shown by the Harvard Modern Art Society. . . . I had a minute when I got back to Boston, so I dropped into the Doll and Richards Galleries to see an exhibition of O'Hara's watercolors—he uses lovely fresh colors.*[2]

Even then, Nelson Rockefeller was approaching art as he approached most other things—with gusto and an almost superhuman energy.

In addition to Rockefeller's schooling, the family environment provided important exposure to art and the impetus to collect it. Through his father, John D. Rockefeller, Jr., Nelson was exposed to the more formal and classical art of the masters and the well-established art of Europe and Asia. As well as being a collector, his father put a great deal of his energy toward art philanthropy, most notably the restorations of the Cloisters, Versailles and Colonial Williamsburg.

It is clear, however, that Nelson's strongest feelings about art came through his mother, Abby Aldrich Rockefeller. In his own words, "The major influence in my life as a collector was my mother. She, in turn, got this interest from her father, Senator Nelson Aldrich, and she spent her life assembling a collection that evolved with her tastes. I think she would have been classified as one of the avant-garde collectors in her day."[3] Abby Aldrich Rockefeller was willing to trust her intuitive response to works of art. She sought out new painters and sculptors who were the bold spokesmen of their era and collected, among other things, primitive art, American folk art and Japanese prints. At home, Abby Rockefeller installed a changing gallery on the upstairs floor of their West Fifty-fourth Street town house. Later, Nelson would do likewise in his own homes. He clearly resembled his

Abby Aldrich Rockefeller, mother of Nelson A. Rockefeller, ca. 1915.

mother physically and in temperament and inherited her unbridled enthusiasm for art, particularly art that was not in the mainstream.

An energetic and creative supporter of public art institutions, Mrs. Rockefeller was the most influential of the three initial founders of the Museum of Modern Art, which opened to the public in November 1929. Her objective for the new museum was "to reduce dramatically the time lag between the artist's creation and the public's approval of great works of art."[4] She also restored Bassett Hall at Colonial Williamsburg and filled it with pieces of American folk art that she and her husband had purchased. When the Folk Art Center at Williamsburg bearing Abby Aldrich Rockefeller's name opened in 1957, it housed 424 splendid examples of American folk art that she had collected from 1929 to 1942.[5]

Abby Rockefeller took pleasure in a shared affinity for art with Nelson, reflected in several letters between them. Early in 1928, while Nelson was still at Dartmouth, he enthusiastically described a weekend he had spent with her in New York:

> Dear Ma,
>
> You don't know how much I enjoyed our two trips to Mr. [Arthur B.] Davies and the visit to the Down Town Galleries. I feel as if I had been introduced to a new world of beauty, and for the first time I think I have really been able to appreciate and understand pictures even though only a little bit. I hope to continue this when I am in New York and maybe do a tiny bit of collecting myself. I feel that was the outstanding event of my vacation.[6]

Shortly afterward, his mother replied:

> It would be a great joy to me if you did find you had a real love for and interest in beautiful things. We could have such a good time going about together, and if you start to cultivate your taste and eye so young, you ought to be very good at it by the time you can afford to collect much. To me art is one of the great resources of my life. I feel that it enriches the spiritual life and makes one more sane and sympathetic, more observant and understanding, as well as being good for one's nerves.[7]

Clearly, Abby Rockefeller's influence on her son's interest in art was profound. Of particular importance to the formation of Nelson Rockefeller's Mexican folk art collection, however, is the role she played in introducing Nelson to the art of Latin America, especially that of Mexico.

Abby Rockefeller's interest in Mexican art grew out of a visit in early 1928 to an exhibition of Mexican fine and applied arts at the Art Center, a New York organization formed by the General Education Board, an entity that, in turn, had been founded in 1902 by John D. Rockefeller, Sr., to improve the quality of education in the United States. Abby Rockefeller visited the exhibition on four occasions and bought a number of pieces, primarily pottery and tiles, which she installed in one of the houses at the family's Pocantico Hills estate.

The exhibition was organized by Frances Flynn Paine, a Texas-born woman who had spent many of her formative years in Mexico and had, early on, been fascinated by the fine craftsmanship of Mexican Indians.[8] She subsequently was given $15,000 by the Rockefeller Foundation to conduct research on Mexican folk art, set up a cooperative among Mexican folk artists and market their goods in the United States. Through Frances Paine, Abby Rockefeller continued to purchase Mexican folk art for herself and her friends. She also commissioned Paine to purchase Spanish colonial furniture and decorative pieces in Mexico for Colonial Williamsburg, feeling that including pieces similar to ones that had been brought to Williamsburg by ship in the early days from other colonies in the Americas would make the collection more authentic. And, with her, she set up the Mexican Arts Association in New York, with initial funding from John D. Rockefeller, Jr. The association's primary purpose was to "promote friendship between the people of Mexico and the United States of America by encouraging cultural relations and the interchange of fine and applied arts [folk art]."[9]

One of the first projects developed by this group was a major retrospective of the work of the Mexican painter Diego Rivera, at the newly formed Museum of Modern Art. It opened on December 23, 1931, as the second one-man show to be held at the museum (the first was of Matisse's work). The exhibition displayed 150 of Rivera's most important works, including oils, watercolors, drawings and frescoes. Some of the frescoes were made specially for the show. Included in this enormously popular and historically important show was Rivera's notebook of Russian May Day sketches, which Abby Rockefeller had purchased for her own collection through Paine and which she later donated to the museum. It was during this period that Abby Rockefeller became a strong benefactor of Rivera and a good friend to Rivera's exotic wife, the artist Frida Kahlo—despite Rivera's much publicized communist sympathies.

Abby Rockefeller's involvement in Mexican art was most intense at precisely the same time young Nelson was developing his own likes and dislikes. Not only did she introduce him to Mexican art, but she also instilled in him a confidence to follow his own instincts and, by her example, taught him that there was valuable artistic expression well beyond the walls of the "safe" art fields of his time.

Nelson Rockefeller's iconoclastic trajectory in art was now set. Although no other person would influence that direction quite as much as his mother, others did assist in adding depth to his artistic commitments. Wallace K. Harrison, a brilliant architect who became a close friend of Rockefeller's, had a tremendous impact on his life in terms of "understanding the relation between the cultural creations of our times and the environment from which they spring."[10] Another such friend was René d'Harnoncourt, an Austrian who had studied pre-Columbian and folk art in Mexico during the late 1920s. D'Harnoncourt later became director of the Museum of Modern Art and a staunch ally in Rockefeller's battle to gain recognition and respect for primitive and folk art. Together, they traveled throughout Latin America and other parts of the world and spent hundreds of hours poring over exotic art from distant cultures and discussing its merits and meanings.

Finally, there were certain events that would build on the foundation laid down by Nelson Rockefeller's mother. Most notable were his early travels abroad, especially during the early 1930s. Nelson married Mary Todhunter Clark in 1930, and his parents gave the young couple a nine-month trip around the world as a wedding gift. They attended native feasts in Hawaii, rode elephants in Indochina, enjoyed folk puppets in Japan and toured the great temples of India. Rockefeller was greatly touched by the warmth and beauty of the people he met and tremendously impressed by their performing and visual arts. It was during this trip that Nelson put into practice some of the strategies of collecting that he had learned from his mother. Among the pieces he purchased were a simple wooden poi bowl from Hawaii, a graceful lute from Sumatra and a seated wooden figure from Bali.

Of particular interest was an introduction in Bali to Miguel Covarrubias, probably arranged through his mother, who had known Covarrubias earlier in New York. The well-known Mexican illustrator, writer and amateur archaeologist was in Bali to write a book on Balinese culture and society—a book that has become recognized as a classic in the study of that part of the world. Covarrubias and his wife, Rosa, encouraged the Rockefellers to visit them in Mexico.

From these early experiences came a deep interest in art, which Rockefeller used personally in his private collecting, publicly in his sponsorship of artists and great museums and diplomatically in his never-ending struggle for better international understanding. The myriad influences of those early days led him to develop not only a keen eye for art but also a personal philosophy that governed his attitude toward art. Rockefeller applied this informal philosophy to all of his great collections—modern, primitive and folk—which he saw as tightly connected to one another.

For Nelson Rockefeller, art was a truly great pinnacle of man's achievement and the purest expression of human energy, creativity and spirituality. He felt that art was "a source of faith and hope, of inspiration to people throughout the world,"[11] and that the power of art could be felt, captured if you will, and enjoyed by all those who partook of it. His interest was in the object of art itself, not in its contextual importance, period or investment potential. In his own words, his interest was "not an intellectual one. It is strictly aesthetic. . . . I enjoy the form, the texture, the color, the shape."[12]

Shortly after returning from his honeymoon, Nelson became a vice president and director of Rockefeller Center, the "city within a city" being built by his father in central Manhattan. The center was to be a showplace for American free enterprise and was designed to feature murals and sculptures of many of the world's greatest living artists. Diego Rivera had been invited to paint the central panel for Thirty Rockefeller Plaza, the center's main structure. (Picasso and Matisse had been approached; both had declined.[13])

At the time he received the commission, Rivera was working on a series of large frescoes at the Detroit Institute of Art, his Maecenas in this case being Edsel Ford.[14] Rivera worked on the project for more than a year, and when, in March 1933, the frescoes were officially unveiled, they immediately provoked tremendous controversy. As Bertram D. Wolfe, a friend of Rivera's, writes in his life of the artist: "The vaccination panel dedicated to the glorification of scientific research . . . aroused particular ire because of its reminiscence of the Holy Family; the stalwart child held by the 'halo'-crowned nurse, being vaccinated by a physician, suggested Mary, Joseph and the Child; the horse, ox and sheep, whence the serum is derived, carried overtones of the stable of the Nativity; the three scientists working in the background were three Magi bearing gifts."[15] The controversy in Detroit proved to be a warning of things to come.

As soon as he had finished work in Detroit, Rivera came to New York, where several young artists, including Ben Shahn, had started preparing the walls at Thirty Rockefeller Plaza. Rivera had less than two months to complete a mural that would cover more than one thousand square feet. Rockefeller Center officials had provided the artist with a theme: "Man at the Crossroads Looking with Hope and High Vision to the Choosing of a New Better Future." Rivera wrote up a detailed description of how he intended to carry out this rather vague assignment and submitted it to the center officials, who gave their approval. May 1 was set as the deadline, because, as Nelson Rockefeller explained to Rivera in a letter written in early April, ". . . the building opens the first of May and it will be tremendously effective to have your mural there to greet the people as they come in for the opening."[16]

As the mural evolved, features that had not been discussed in detail began to emerge; most notably, a central figure Rivera had described merely as "the Worker" or "the labor leader" became a portrait of Lenin. Rivera had joined the Communist Party in 1924, but by the time he came to America, he had resigned from it, been readmitted, and in 1929 been expelled. His expulsion had done nothing to lessen his revolutionary ardor and, Wolfe writes, "the fact that he was painting for a Rockefeller and that the Communist Party was attacking him as a painter for millionaires strengthened his determination to show what a Communist he was."[17]

On May 4, Rockefeller, who had repeatedly been obliged to resolve differences between the painter and the center's chief architect, wrote Rivera, urging him to "substitute the face of some unknown man where Lenin's face now appears."[18] Rivera refused to do so but offered to balance the portrait of Lenin with a similarly strong likeness of Lincoln on the other side of the mural.

Some days later, while Nelson was out of town, officials at the center stopped Rivera's work, paid him in full ($21,500), and covered the mural with cloth. There were protests and demonstrations, but both sides refused to give in. Nelson tried to make arrangements for the unfinished mural to be removed from Rockefeller Center and placed on permanent exhibition at the Museum of Modern Art, but the plan proved to be unworkable. Sadly, Rivera's mural was chipped from the wall in February 1934. It was reproduced in modified form in Mexico City's Palace of Fine Arts.

The Rivera mural episode had greatly shaken Rockefeller. He had worked hard to reach an acceptable compromise, but none had been found. Furthermore, he was upset that the mural, which he thought to be a masterpiece in spite of part of its content, had been destroyed. Forty years later, he lamented that "my mother and I lost ground on the Rivera mural."[19] The controversy had taught young Rockefeller several important lessons. First, it demonstrated the tremendous ability of art, when moved outside of studios, galleries and museums, to become a powerful catalyst for political and social change. Clearly, the Rivera mural was as charged with social and political criticism as any of the moving speeches or printed opinions of the time. It had the power to make people rally in favor of its stance and to drive others into highly charged opposition. It could not be ignored. Second, the incident showed how much of Mexican art was integrated into the everyday life and politics of that nation. Social Art had become a solid part of the New Order in Mexico, and the art community was behind it. When the Rockefeller Plaza dispute erupted, most of the Mexican art community quickly fell in behind Rivera.

Rockefeller did not allow the painful situation to deflect him from pursuing his strong interest in Mexican art. Eventually amends were made, and the friendship with Frida and Diego was renewed. Rockefeller was determined to visit Mexico, a country in which, uniquely, art was helping to reshape the way the nation thought of itself. So, in the summer of 1933, only a few months after the covering of Rivera's mural, Nelson and Mary decided to sail from New York to Veracruz.

MEXICO: A NATION DISCOVERS ITSELF

Mexico in the 1930s was a radically different country than it had been only a decade before, and, artistically, a far more exciting one. The Mexican Revolution of 1910-1921 put an end to the stagnant, corrupt government of dictator Porfirio Díaz; thereafter, the country began looking inward, and into its own past, for symbols and ideals on which to base a new Mexican identity.

During the Díaz era, the upper classes had looked down on native art—if, indeed, they even took notice of it—regarding only European art and culture, and to a lesser extent North American art and culture, as significant. The architecture, sculpture and painting of the era all reflected this basically anti-Mexican bias. An example of this attitude was provided on the occasion of the celebration in 1910 of the centennial of the first uprising against Spanish rule. President Díaz imported an exhibition of Spanish paintings and, in preparation for the festivities, had ordered the construction of a new museum, the Palace of Fine Arts. Amy Conger, an early admirer and collector of Mexican folk art, notes in her book on the American photographer Edward Weston: "The building was designed by Italians, the survey and foundation were carried out by North Americans, the marble statues were carved by a Catalan, the facade sculpture and dome were planned and carried out by Italians, the marble was imported from Carrara and the crystal screen was executed by Tiffany in New York—all while the building rapidly sank into the ground. It was the embodiment of Mexico's cultural inferiority complex."[20]

Weston's tart comment was that Díaz "should have been dethroned for aesthetic reasons, not political. In such a revolution I could joyfully take part!"[21]

In 1921, the year after General Álvaro Obregón, a hero of the revolution, became president of the shaky republic, he appointed humanist and writer José Vasconcelos minister of public education. Daniel Rubín de la Borbolla, a specialist in this period, describes Vasconcelos as being "determined to fulfill part of the mandate of the Mexican Revolution by incorporating the Indian into society, partly through public education and the promotion of the aesthetic accomplishments of Mexicans in Mexico."[22]

The results of this change of attitude on the part of Mexico's leaders were made dramatically manifest in a celebration that was, in effect, a counter-celebration to the one staged by Díaz. Nineteen twenty-one marked the centennial of Mexico's independence. To celebrate this national birthday, the government asked three artists—Jorge Enciso, Roberto Montenegro and Dr. Atl—to put together a first-class collection of popular art from all over the republic and to mount an exhibition in a building on Avenida Juárez, in the center of Mexico City. With this exhibition, officially opened by President Obregón, the government put its new face on display for the first time and declared that the future was to be built on internal strengths and traditions rather than imported ones.

Frances Toor, who became a leader in Mexican folk art research, recalls the effect this show had on her as well as others:

> *I had just come to Mexico City to attend the National University Summer School, when it was shown there and the beauty of it was to be one of the motivating factors in my remaining. I wanted to know more of the country in which such humble people could make such beautiful things.*

The exhibition was a revelation to the Mexicans themselves. Since then, it has become quite the mode among well-to-do Mexican families, especially those connected with the government, to have a Mexican Room, decorated with Indian handy-crafts.[23]

Almost as important as the exhibition itself was the catalogue, written by Dr. Atl, titled *Las Artes Populares en México*. This publication, issued in two volumes, one of text, the other of illustrations, provided a remarkable overview of Mexican popular arts of the 1920s.

In 1922 the Mexican Secretariat of Industry, Commerce and Labor organized another pioneering folk art exhibition—designed this time to travel to Los Angeles. Historians and artists assembled the best objects to be found in village markets and shops. Novelist Katherine Anne Porter wrote the catalogue, titled *Outline of Mexican Arts and Crafts*. It contains original insights into Mexican folk culture, but the prose is steeped in the sort of romantic sensibility that characterized much of the writing on the arts following the revolution. Its chief significance lies in its being the first catalogue on Mexican folk art published in the United States to treat that art as an integral part of Mexican culture.

Several foreigners who were living in Mexico City during the 1920s played major roles in recording, collecting and preserving folk art. Edward Weston traveled about the country photographing folk murals, black pottery from Oaxaca, lacquerware from Michoacán and thousands of other folk art objects. He was captivated by Mexican folk toys, which he described as "major art," "graceful" and "elegant."[24]

Another key participant in the folk art scene was Fred Davis—who, incidentally, initially sponsored René d'Harnoncourt upon his arrival in Mexico as a refugee from Austria in 1927. An American collector and folk art dealer who had moved to Mexico early in the century, Davis had set up one of the first folk art shops of quality in Mexico City. Later, he directed Sanborn's gallery on Avenida Madero. Davis was at the center of a group of writers, collectors, folk art specialists and painters—among them, Roberto Montenegro and Miguel Covarrubias—and, according to d'Harnoncourt's widow, Sarah, Davis belonged to a more specialized group, as well: a band of men who not only studied folk art but also scoured the countryside, looking for new and exciting examples. "They would travel together to faraway Indian villages," she recalls, "and each would try to be the first person up the next morning in order to beat the others to the market for the best pieces."[25] Weston, remembering a trip to Lake Pátzcuaro, confirms this competitive spirit: "That night we overslept, and René beat us to the market, returning in triumph with a water bottle, a fat round little duck—a gem in red clay. Leaving coffee half finished, I scurried to the plaza and bought one—the last, for myself. Later I purchased a bird—a transfigured gourd."[26]

Painter Jean Charlot, who was at the center of Mexico's artistic ferment during this period, remembers:

> In the Mexico of the 1920s, the concept of a fine arts market was still meaningless in terms of a 57th Street of velvet-lined displays. Yet art was everywhere: devotees bribed saints with ex-votos, lovers melted the hearts of their beloved with portraits, artisans and merchants hired the painter to beautify their shops with murals and thus increased business. Sculpture existed for specialized aims—dark pieces, idols of secret worship, semblances used for black magic; innocent pieces, those marvelous toys worth a few cents, beautiful as Han tomb figures. The output was so varied as to be unclassifiable, so cheap as to be despised, so close to all, so thrust under everyone's eyes as to become invisible.[27]

The year 1930 marked yet another milestone in Mexican folk art, particularly in the international arena. Dwight W. Morrow, one of the United States' most beloved and successful ambassadors to Mexico, had a deep appreciation for all forms of Mexican art. So, too, did his wife, Elizabeth, who, with Abby Aldrich Rockefeller, had been a founding member of the Mexican Arts Association in New York. An avid collector of folk art, ancient and contemporary, Morrow had personally underwritten the Rivera murals in the Cortez Palace in Cuernavaca in the late 1920s. Feeling that citizens of the United States knew far too little about the arts of Mexico, he and silver designer William Spratling of Taxco organized a nearly encyclopedic exhibition of Mexican art that traveled to major cities in the United States between 1930 and 1932. Morrow asked d'Harnoncourt to select the objects, write a catalogue and travel with the exhibit, taking charge of the installation at each stop. Following its inauguration in Mexico City on June 25, 1930, the exhibition opened at the Metropolitan Museum of Art in New York in October; its eight-city itinerary ended in San Antonio in September 1931.

In his introduction to the catalogue, titled *Mexican Arts*, d'Harnoncourt explained the parameters of the exhibition:

> *This is an exhibition of Mexican arts, not of arts in Mexico. Many art objects are produced within the physical limits of the Republic that are Mexican only in a geographical sense, but these unassimilated copies of foreign models must be disregarded for the purposes of this exhibition. We are concerned here with the presentation only of such works as are an expression of Mexican civilization.*[28]

The contemporary painters and sculptors whose works were included were those who called on indigenous folk forms, colors and themes for inspiration: Rivera, Covarrubias, Abraham Angel, Julio Castellanos, Carlos Mérida and others. The exhibition displays, all designed by d'Harnoncourt, were spectacular. Sixteenth-century feather mosaic portraits, *retablos*, *milagros*, early and contemporary dance masks, textiles of every color and texture and lacquerware were included—each the finest examples available in its particular medium. Pottery from all over Mexico, old and new furniture, glassware and dozens of other types of objects, all displayed with originality and charm, made this exhibition the talk of the art world. In addition to the scope and quality of the folk art it presented to the American public, the show was significant in that it made the strongest statement yet on the art of the Mexican Renaissance and its importance in establishing a national identity.

Mildred Constantine, a keen observer of the Mexican art movement of the 1930s, states that "art took its proper place with politics and other things. Mexico was full of ferment—part art and part politics. There was a tremendous cohesion in Mexico in those days among poets, painters, and writers."[29] They were all participants in the Mexican Renaissance; they all directed much of their energy toward achieving the goals of the Mexican Revolution—bettering the lot of the masses who had been overlooked by the previous regime. Art had been taken out of the rarified climates of galleries and museums; instead of drawing from European models, it looked inward to pre-Columbian and folk art to build a new identity. Constantine recalls, "The same people who were painting posters against illiteracy were painting murals. The *zócalo* [main plaza] was theater in action, and each day people came in from the countryside to see the great murals which chronicled their struggles."[30]

VOYAGE TO MEXICO

The Rockefellers sailed from New York for Veracruz on July 26, 1933, by way of Havana. Their itinerary had been set up by Frances Flynn Paine, who also served as their guide throughout the trips. Charles R. Richards, director of the art section of the General Education Board, described her special qualifications for dealing with folk societies:

> *Since first meeting Mrs. Paine. . . I have come to know her somewhat intimately and find that she is a woman of much quiet power and resolution, with a fine mind and a deep and abiding interest in the welfare and in the arts of the Indians of Mexico. She was born in Laredo, Texas, but spent most of her early days in Mexico, where her father was for a time Superintendent of Railways and also acted at times as American Consul. He was a man who possessed, I understand, mining and agricultural interests in various parts of Mexico and to these various places Mrs. Paine traveled when she was quite young, living in many remote parts of Mexico. It was during this period that she first conceived her interest in the crafts of the Mexican Indians. As a consequence, she possessed a knowledge of these crafts, as well as an intimate knowledge of the Indian character, that has developed steadily during her almost life-long residence in Mexico.*[31]

Paine had arranged for the Rockefellers to see some of the great collections of pre-Columbian art in Mexico, among them those belonging to Miguel and Rosa Covarrubias. Nelson recalled that, "I found myself captivated by the power and exquisite refinement of these works. It was a most exciting and exhilarating experience, opening up new worlds—worlds little known and little appreciated at that time outside of Latin America and anthropological circles."[32] Many of Mexico's artists and writers lived with the art of their ancestors as well as folk art produced by contemporary Indians. For the first time, Rockefeller had the opportunity to see these objects and to talk with collectors about the availability of folk art and the context in which it was being produced and used.

While he was awed by the pre-Columbian art he saw on this trip, it was folk art—and the people who made and used it—that made the deepest impression on him. The Rockefellers traveled through the central highlands of Mexico, in and out of shops and museums in Mexico City and into the states of Puebla and Morelos to visit old churches, many of them

Frances Flynn Paine, second from left, who guided the Rockefellers on their first trip to Mexico. She is with, from right to left, Diego Rivera, Elie Faure, Jean Charlot, Frida Kahlo and Dr. Leo Eloesoer. This photograph was taken in August 1931 at Cuernavaca on the portal of the Cortez Palace, where Rivera painted frescoes depicting the Conquest of Mexico. These frescoes were commissioned by Ambassador Dwight Morrow as a gift to the State of Morelos.

embellished with folk sculpture and paintings. Forty-five years later, reflecting on this trip, Nelson recalled that he and Mary were uniquely privileged to travel with Frances Paine from marketplace to marketplace.[33]

Rockefeller distinctly remembered several of the folk artists he met on that first trip to Mexico. One was an elderly Indian woman who wove sarapes in a village in the State of Tlaxcala. Her "weaving was so fine that no one of the younger generation had the patience to develop the skills required to carry it on," he recalled. "I was so excited by her wonderful work that I bought virtually her entire collection. . . . I have never found anything to compare with the work of that beautiful and gentle little lady who was so pleased by the joy we derived from her works."[34]

Another artist who made a lasting impression on Rockefeller was an Indian sculptor named Mardonio Magaña, from Mexico City. "We first saw one of his works in a square near the San Angel Inn. . . . This piece of sculpture evidenced such sensitivity and humanity, as well as artistic quality, that I asked Mrs. Paine if she could make arrangements for a visit to his studio. Magaña was as beautiful and gentle as his sculpture. Without hesitation, I bought two of his stone pieces and two wood carvings, each of which manifested the same deep love and sensitive human understanding of the Mexican campesino that I had found in his larger piece in the square."[35] In Magaña's work, Rockefeller found a combination of pre-Hispanic and folk forms redirected into modern forms of expression.

Paine also introduced Rockefeller to Roberto Montenegro, a portrait painter and muralist and an avid collector and student of folk art. Later, it would be Montenegro who would lead Rockefeller more deeply into folk art. Like many of the other great Mexican artists of that period, Montenegro looked to the folk art of his country for inspiration and was vitally interested in its recognition and preservation. In 1922 he organized Mexico's first popular arts exhibit in the United States and subsequently set up the Museo de Artes Populares in Mexico City. Rockefeller chose Montenegro to head up the folk art section of the Museum of Modern Art's pioneering 1940 exhibition of Mexican art.

Nelson and Mary returned to New York at the end of August. He had purchased Mexican art of all types, including pre-Columbian and colonial pieces and contemporary paintings and sculpture. But most of the twenty-six crates of art he shipped back were filled with folk art. Some of these pieces had been bought from collectors such as Covarrubias and Montenegro; others at Fred Davis' legendary folk art shop in Mexico City. The great majority of the pieces of the folk art had been bought directly from the artists who had created them. This human connection made these works special to Nelson.

Rockefeller made several other trips to Mexico during the 1930s. Each visit reinforced his interest in folk art. In 1939 he became president of the Museum of Modern Art and immediately set about organizing a major exhibition of Mexican art. He went to Mexico to meet with President Lázaro Cárdenas, who agreed to co-sponsor the event and share in the expenses. He chose leading authorities in the field to head each of the four sections of the exhibition. Alfonso Caso, Mexico's dean of archaeology, was put in charge of the pre-Columbian section; Manuel Toussaint, of the colonial material; Miguel Covarrubias, of modern art; and Roberto Montenegro, of folk art. The show, called *20 Centuries of Mexican Art*, bringing together two thousand masterpieces from these various periods, was the most extensive survey of Mexican art ever presented outside of Mexico.

To build a great collection of Mexican popular arts for the exhibition, Rockefeller commissioned Montenegro to travel about the Mexican countryside to purchase old and new folk art. This was done with the understanding that the works would become part of Rockefeller's private collection once the show was over. Some of the rarest and most important pieces in the Rockefeller collection are those purchased by Montenegro for the *20 Centuries* exhibition.

In addition to rare and historically important pieces of folk art, everyday contemporary crafts were also purchased and used in a replica of a Mexican marketplace that was constructed in the garden of the Museum of Modern Art for their display and sale. The exhibition was a tremendous success;

after it closed, the folk art section traveled to museums throughout the United States under the auspices of the Museum of Modern Art.

Rockefeller's motivations for supporting the *20 Centuries of Mexican Art* project were twofold. First, he was attracted to the works and believed in their artistic value. Second, he saw the exhibition as an excellent opportunity to shore up relations between Mexico and the United States. Opening at about the same time that President Roosevelt appointed him to the post of Coordinator for Inter-American Affairs, the show was an initial expression of his commitment to inter-American cooperation. Because of his interest in the cultural-exchange aspect of the project, he saw it as an opportunity for the Mexican government to set up markets in the United States for Mexican folk art and crafts. Rockefeller was elated, for example, when he learned that Kaufman's Department Store in Pittsburgh had decided to launch a major merchandising campaign featuring popular Mexican crafts and other objects, basing its decision on the publicity generated by the

Rockefeller at a party in Mexico City, with Frida Kahlo on his left and Rosa Covarrubias on his right, mid-1940s.

Museum of Modern Art's exhibit. William Spratling, who revived the silver arts in Taxco, writes that Rockefeller worked hard in the 1940s to lower United States silver tariffs, to improve trade relations between the United States and Mexico.[36] Rockefeller saw these kinds of responses as important steps in strengthening economic ties with Latin American republics at a time when such ties were tenuous at best.

During World War II, while working for the Roosevelt administration, Rockefeller continued to travel to Mexico and other parts of Latin America—and, whenever he had free time, he collected folk art. Susan Herter, who served as an assistant to Rockefeller during that period, remembers that "in 1945 in Mexico City during the Chapultepec conference to revitalize hemispheric unity, Rockefeller would often disappear at breaks and at lunchtime. He was out seeking new pieces for his growing collection and was greatly excited with his finds; he gave many wonderful pieces away when they were admired by friends and visitors."[37]

After the war, Rockefeller kept in close contact with Mexican politics, development programs, and art. In 1948, feeling that he had been away from folk art too long, he decided to take his wife and five children to Mexico for several weeks of vacation.

The Rockefeller family flew to Mexico City on June 20. They dropped in for a visit with their friends Rosa and Miguel Covarrubias, in whose home the family admired the couple's splendid collections of pre-Columbian and folk art.

Roberto Montenegro was to be the family's guide on this trip, and after much discussion and debate, Oaxaca was chosen as the destination, presumably because it would provide an ideal spot to give the Rockefeller children an overview of Mexican art in one locale. Within the Valley of Oaxaca the ruins of Monte Albán and Mitla provided constant reminders of the antiquity and early splendor of the region. Then, too, there were the Spanish colonial churches—two hundred years older than the earliest North American churches—richly decorated with sixteenth-century frescoes and gold-leafed walls and ceilings. And, of course, every village in the region produced folk art of some type, much of it marketed in the main square of Oaxaca City.

Rockefeller with Miguel and Rosa Covarrubias in Mexico City, mid-1940s.

From left to right: Nelson A. Rockefeller; Rosa Covarrubias; William Spratling, the designer who revived the silver industry in Taxco; and Roberto Montenegro, in Mexico City, mid-1940s.

In those days the outdoor Oaxaca market encompassed dozens of square blocks in the center of the city. One needed only to sit for a brief time on a nearby bench in order to see hundreds of colorfully dressed Indians, Mixtecs, Zapotecs, Triques and others from the mountains surrounding the Valley of Oaxaca—bringing their wares to market to sell or exchange for items not available in their home communities. Oaxaca was the ideal place to see many of Mexico's most dramatic elements all at once.

The Rockefellers visited dozens of villages in the Valley of Oaxaca, and his elder daughter, Ann R. Roberts, recalls "the excitement and fascination of going in and out of the homes of artisans with Father—going in empty-handed and coming out with little treasures."[38]

The family ended their Mexican trip with a visit to Tehuantepec, about 150 miles south of Oaxaca City. Miguel Covarrubias had just published a major study of the Tehuantepec region, and this influenced Rockefeller's decision to include this stop in the itinerary. Tropical and filled with exotic flowers and birds, Tehuantepec provided a vivid contrast to the semiarid Valley of Oaxaca. There they saw Zapotec and Huave Indian women skill-fully running markets offering for sale exotic regional specialties such as iguana cooked in a red sauce and eaten on a tortilla, richly lacquered bowls used in fiestas and textiles dyed purple with the secretions from a local shellfish gathered by the nearby Chontal Indians. This southern foray also gave the family an opportunity to visit San Blas Atempa, a Zapotec village famous for its ceramics, especially large figural pieces used as water-container supports.

Montenegro was in his element and added enormously to the success of the trip. Mary Rockefeller recalls that "Roberto made an enormous impres-sion on Nelson. Not only was he very knowledgeable about folk art, but he also enjoyed a special rapport with folk artists and delighted in being with them in their homes. Nelson found Roberto's enthusiasm contagious and soon he was reacting to folk art in a similar fashion."[39] Roberto became a close family friend, and correspondence between him and Nelson continued until Montenegro's death in 1968.

Roberto Montenegro with his portrait of fellow artist José Clemente Orozco in 1949.

As Rockefeller became more deeply involved in domestic politics, his involvement with Mexican art and culture diminished. During his long tenure as governor of New York from 1959 to 1973, he had little opportunity to visit Latin America and the Indian markets he loved so much. But in 1968 his interest in Mexican folk art was rekindled when, quite by accident, he happened upon a small and colorful folk art gallery/shop in Manhattan called the Mexican Folk Art Annex. It was owned and run by Annie O'Neill, an artist with an effervescent personality and a good eye for folk art. O'Neill recalls her first meeting with Rockefeller, who would later employ her as a folk art consultant.

> I still clearly remember his first visit. It was after five o'clock and the shop was closed. When I looked through the peephole to decide whether or not to let one last person in, I thought that I had better let that tired-looking man come in. What a surprise to discover he was the governor! An even greater treat was to watch him voraciously assimilate everything on all the shelves and in every corner. After a few minutes he looked like a different person—he had been energized.[40]

Part of the exhibition of Mexican folk art in the Museum of Primitive Art in 1969. Rockefeller often encouraged a market flavor in the installation of his folk art collection.

Shortly after this chance encounter, Rockefeller started unpacking all of the old crates of folk art left over from the *20 Centuries of Mexican Art* exhibition and began planning a new folk art exhibit at the Museum of Primitive Art. O'Neill was dispatched immediately to Mexico to make additional purchases to fill in gaps in the collection. Carl Fox, a folk art specialist who had worked with the Smithsonian Institution and the Brooklyn Museum, was hired to design the exhibition and assemble a catalogue. The exhibition opened on May 21, 1969. Its success with the public pleased Rockefeller enormously.

In his foreword to the catalogue, he wrote:

> It does not matter if these [objects] are categorized as "minor" arts. Artificial categories disappear before works whose vivid color and spontaneous design reflect such pleasure in their making. They delight and fascinate us—and happily let us share in the vitality and love that went into their creation.[41]

Rockefeller continued collecting and studying Mexican folk art well into the 1970s. When he became vice president of the United States in 1974, he was again drawn away from his collections. But, in 1977, he returned to New York and the family offices, where he worked almost daily on projects related to art. A year later, he announced plans to publish a series of five books on his art collections. One of these was to concentrate on his Mexican folk art collection. As part of this project he decided to visit Mexico again, to photograph folk artists, make new purchases and visit old haunts.

Rockefeller asked several friends to accompany him, including Carl Fox, Annie O'Neill and art photographer Lee Boltin. Another member of this group was Rockefeller's daughter Ann, who inherited her father's love of folk art and who, after his death, arranged for his Mexican folk art collection to be preserved and placed in new and permanent homes.

In 1978 Rockefeller returned to Oaxaca, where he had spent such a pleasant time with his family thirty years before. Moreover, in what was to be the last year of his life, he arranged to be there in early November for the preparations of the Day of the Dead—a three-day religious festival lasting from October 31 to November 2, All Souls' Day. It is a time of year when folk art is most visible and abundant. In his biography of Diego Rivera, Bertram Wolfe writes of "the mordant-reckless-festive-friendly-familiar Mexican attitude toward death,"[42] an attitude made fantastically manifest during this festival, when death is at once mocked and honored. In every city and village, families go out to the cemeteries, carrying flowers, sweets, food and drink to the graves of the dead. Children make cardboard skeletons dance and amuse themselves with little figures of death made of metal foil, with chick-peas serving as heads, or with small coffins made of cardboard or clay. Death is also eaten in the form of sugar-candy skulls or figures made of sugar or marzipan.

Shortly after arriving in Oaxaca, the group set off to visit the great figural ceramist Doña Teodora Blanco in the village of Santa María Atzompa. Rockefeller was captivated by the woman, by her work and by the way she worked. "She is a person of such an active mind," he later wrote, "so feeling and creative that one thought leads to another and each is expressed in sculptural form through some additions to or elaboration of the piece in hand—with lightning speed and sensitivity."[43]

He spent two hours with Doña Teodora, talking with her about her life, photographing her at work and enjoying the ambience of her open-air workshop—with babies crying, animals moving about and shade trees providing shelter from the sun. He purchased everything she was willing to sell, even old broken pieces that Doña Teodora had discarded. Her works, Rockefeller later recalled, ranged in price "from a few cents to less than a hundred dollars for her largest monumental piece, [and yet,] aesthetically, they represented a subtle sophistication possessed by but few of the greatest contemporary artists."[44]

Later, Rockefeller and his companions drove to San Bartolo Coyotepec to visit the legendary Doña Rosa Real de Nieto in her home, where he admired the black pottery for which she and her family are renowned. He bought many pieces from Doña Rosa to complement others he had bought in the 1940s. He also visited the home of the Aguilar family in Ocotlán de Morelos to watch as pottery figures were sculpted and painted. While there, he noticed an assortment of old ceramic figures, some broken, all faded, which had been stuck on the fence posts surrounding the Aguilar home to advertise their business. Noting the special charm of these forgotten pieces, Rockefeller purchased nearly all of them; today they comprise an important part of the figural ceramics in the collection.

The group also visited several large markets while in Oaxaca, including that in Ocotlán de Morelos. Rockefeller plunged right into the middle of the activity. Ocotlán, he remembered, "was alive with Indians, the men wearing big hats, coming and going, picking their way through the crowds, buying and selling, while the women sat quietly, weaving raffia, embroidering, feeding their babies and enjoying the hustle and bustle of this important weekly social event."[45]

Again, he bought whatever impressed him as beautiful and interesting. When he noticed the graceful lines of a handmade ox yoke, he struck a deal with its owner and had it lugged off to a waiting van. He bought small clay whistles, tinsel-covered candles, Day of the Dead bread and wooden combs. He even purchased great wreaths of garlic—much to the dismay of those who were traveling with him.

Teodora Blanco talking about her work with Rockefeller, Santa María Atzompa, Oaxaca, October 1978.

Plate 1
Ceramic Dolls
Mezcala region, Guerrero.
1930s.
Hand-built, single-fired
earthenware, approximate heights,
18". MM and SAMA.

These stately hand-built figures,
painted in earth tones over a creamy
white wash, are disappearing from
the indigenous Mezcala region
figural repertoire. They are being
replaced by gaudily decorated ceramic dolls painted for the tourist
trade. These unusually shaped dolls,
with imploring eyes and head
shapes reminiscent of pre-Hispanic
figurative pieces, reflect an
innovative treatment of the
mother-and-child theme. The
simple floral and animal motifs are
characteristic of the painting in the
early decades of the twentieth
century.

A PHILOSOPHY OF COLLECTING

Rockefeller's relationship to art was very personal and, almost always, emotionally charged. He felt that "art fulfilled a spiritual need in our over-mechanized industrial age," and added that "twentieth-century man is so surrounded by mass-production, by machines and anonymous consumer goods that his eye thirsts for individuality. He turns to art to enjoy individual expression. Paintings and sculpture, artifacts created by individual hands and conceived by individual spirits, satisfy a craving for personality, for uniqueness."[46]

For the most part, Rockefeller tended to avoid highly representational art and art that gave the viewer everything at once, and only once. Instead, he proclaimed that what we are all looking for is something "that takes us out of ourselves and gives us the kind of excitement, the kind of aesthetic satisfaction and challenge that is unending and from which you constantly get new satisfaction and rewards."[47] He felt that a good piece of art, whether it be folk, modern or primitive, would continue to give the viewer a sense of something new and exciting—a new shape, texture or color, and that this would, in turn, be a true reflection of the artist's own evolving qualities. He was particularly drawn to pieces that he felt were direct expressions of strong emotions, pieces made by special artists to be found in every society, no matter what its level of development. "I have always liked forms of art in which I could feel—feel the artists, feel the material."[48]

The direct expressiveness he saw in folk art and certain primitive pieces was shared by some of the great modernists, such as Pablo Picasso. Rockefeller agreed with Gertrude Stein, the author and great collector of modern art, when she wrote that before Picasso, with the exception of the creators of some African sculpture, "no one had ever tried to express things seen not as one knows them but as they are when one sees them without remembering having looked at them."[49] Rockefeller responded to this directness and used it as a guideline for his collecting.

He felt that each of the areas in which he collected was related to the others and that each had something of value to offer the other. He strongly

Rockefeller completing his sombrero purchase in Ocotlán, October 1978.

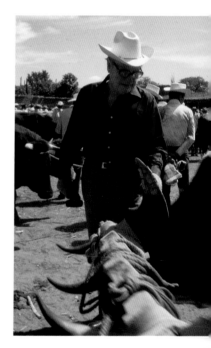

Rockefeller considering buying an ox yoke in the crowded Ocotlán animal market, October 1978.

Doña Rosa at right, working clay, and at left, at work with her son. They both use small kick wheels. San Bartolo Coyotepec, Oaxaca, October 1978.

believed that the "so-called primitive artist, in his economical and varied use of homely materials—sea shells, feathers, bark cloth, straw and bone—can still teach his modernist colleagues a good deal." And one reviewer adds, "No doubt it is Rockefeller's recognition of that fact [of closeness] that explains his interest in folk art and that sends him rummaging in foreign bazaars and second-story craft shops where collectors concerned only with the prestige of a price tag would never venture."[50]

Rockefeller's unorthodox manner of collecting reflected his attitude toward art. He always knew exactly what he liked and acted on his likes very quickly, without stopping to consider the overall significance of a purchase. According to Laurance Rockefeller, "Nelson's reaction to art was visceral," and he had great confidence in his good eye and natural feeling for art. "Collecting," he adds, "gave Nelson a sense of solace and allowed him to get out of the world of day-to-day problems into the quieter dimension of art."[51]

Alfred Barr, former director of the Museum of Modern Art and longtime close friend of Rockefeller's, stated that "Nelson had the most insatiable appetite for art I know. Works of art gave him a deep, almost therapeutic delight and refreshment such as other men may find in music or alcohol."[52]

René d'Harnoncourt, who collected art all over the world with Rocke-feller, observed that "Nelson takes things in like a sponge . . . he reacted strongly to all objects of art and was remarkably free from prejudice. The kind of euphoria he received had nothing to do with that gambler's excitement characteristic of many collectors. It was not unlike benzedrine, it was a curious combination of excitement and relaxation. Call it solace, call it therapy. . . . Most men, after a hard day's work, want to relax. But Nelson was a man of such physical and intellectual energy that he preferred to go on working. . . . I mean by that, it is very hard work to look at paintings and sculpture as intensely as he does. One simply feels he enjoyed himself more profoundly, when he looked at art, than in any other activity."[53]

Rockefeller's collecting habits and the motivations behind them were unusual in the world of art. Barr sees his motives in collecting as being "exceptionally pure. Status, competition, investment, pride of possession, pride of taste, even a reputation for being a 'patron of the arts' did not interest him. Yet, beyond his private satisfaction there was a strong desire to share his treasures with others."[54] Rockefeller quickly dismissed the suggestion that he was building his collection for investment purposes and stated emphatically that "I could be just as happy collecting in a market in Mexico City in the early 1930s as I could in a gallery. It hasn't anything to do with monetary value."[55]

Rockefeller enjoyed the process of collecting immensely, especially amid the bustle and confusion found in a Mexican market. "He loved the physical and emotional contact a marketplace is all about," recalls Annie O'Neill. Again, reflecting on that last trip to Oaxaca, O'Neill says that "whenever Rockefeller bought a piece of art, he underwent a very personal experience. For him, the object had everything to do with the artisans, their pride and dignity, the transaction and the setting."[56]

Rockefeller always traveled with a camera so that he could capture a part of what he liked of the people and places he visited. During the 1978 trip, he took over 150 photographs, many of which deal with village life in Oaxaca. Many of them are of crowded market scenes and folk artists from Ocotlán and Coyotepec. They show women sitting on the ground behind neatly stacked piles of fresh fruit or hanging baskets and petals, or men tugging at animals reluctant to go on the selling block. Most photographs are taken from a spot central to the action and show that the photographer was surrounded on all sides by vendors, buyers and merchandise. Very seldom did he photograph folk art objects by themselves, choosing to focus instead on the people who made, sold and used them.

Rockefeller and his entourage returned to New York in early November. Work on the book began almost immediately. Objects were photographed and preliminary plans were drawn up for the organization of the book. Sadly, Nelson Rockefeller died only three months after returning from Oaxaca, and the folk art project was halted.

Fortunately, an important part of Nelson Rockefeller lives on through his Mexican folk art collection and his other collections of art. These collections reflect his constant faith in the inherent creativity of all people, regardless of cultural background or socioeconomic circumstance. His collecting, out of step with most of his peers, was directed not by fashion, price or potential market value but by the intrinsic beauty and charm he recognized in the pieces themselves. He trusted his emotional response to art, and as the world now knows, he was usually right.

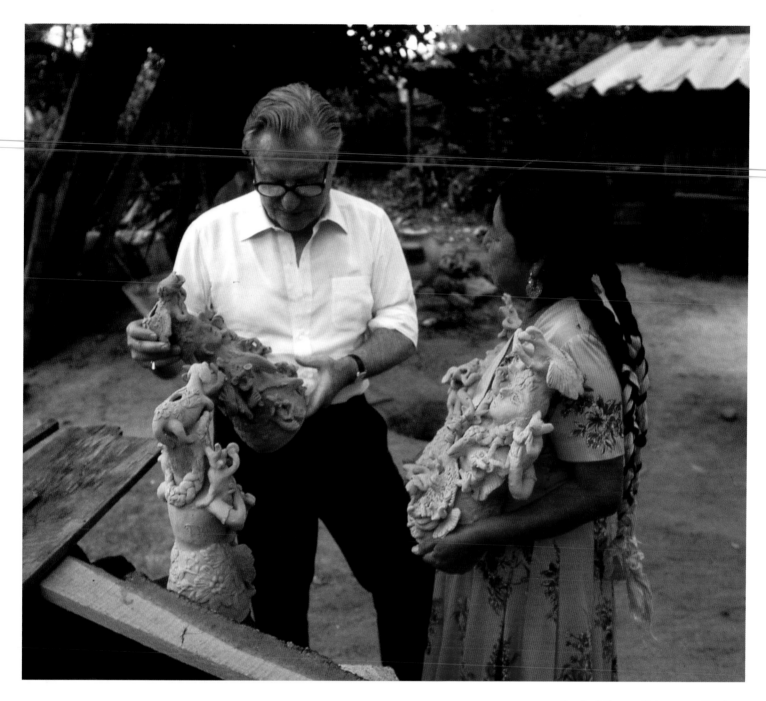

Rockefeller talking to Teodora Blanco about her work at her home in Santa María Atzompa, Oaxaca, October 1978.

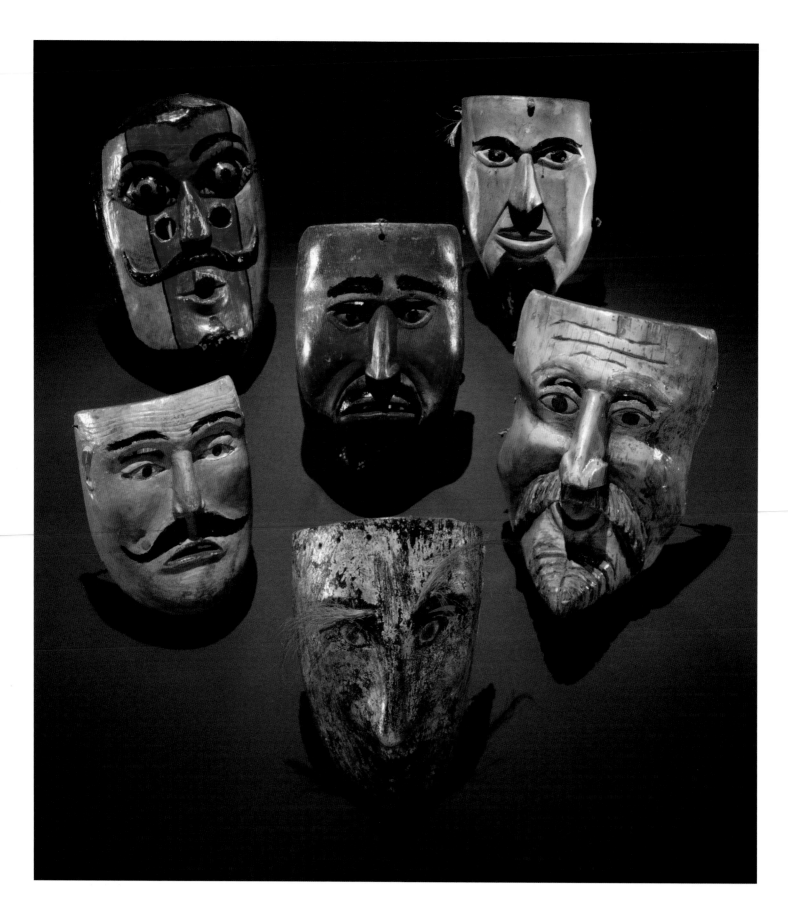

The Collection

Here is an art, almost unknown in the world today, a survival from internal wars, conquests, many fusions; an actual thing full of breathing vitality and meaning.

—Katherine Anne Porter[1]

Nelson Rockefeller's collection of Mexican folk art is both broad and varied. Parts of it are intensely personal and reveal Rockefeller's spontaneous collecting habits and lack of concern for representing all categories or for meeting a curator's stringent criteria. Other works—particularly the large number assembled by Roberto Montenegro for the 1940 Museum of Modern Art exhibition *20 Centuries of Mexican Art*—demonstrate a commitment to covering major historical, geographical and topological areas of Mexican folk art.

The collection comprises objects ranging from colorful toys that dance and tumble, to sedate religious icons that tug at the soul. It contains objects of everyday use, with cool simple lines, and others whose warmth invites our touch. There are objects that represent love, hate, life, death and many other states of the human condition. It is a collection that, when properly understood, reveals an important part of the essence of Mexican society and culture.

HISTORY AND IMPORTANCE OF THE COLLECTION

Beginning in 1933, with Rockefeller's first trip to Mexico, the collection grew over the years at an uneven pace, with inter-American politics, special museum exhibitions and Rockefeller's periodic rekindling of interest in folk

Plate 2
Masks.
Various states of Mexico.
1920s to 1930s.
Painted wood, heights, 12½".
MM and SAMA

Modern masking in Mexico is firmly rooted in pre-Hispanic and colonial times. It can be found in most parts of Mexico and is an essential part of dance dramas dealing with moral and historical themes in celebration of important saint days and other religious events. Mask makers are primarily men; for its creator, mask making is often a fulfillment of a religious obligation to the community. Some masks are destroyed after the ceremony they are used for, while other masks are repainted each year. In some areas, such as Guerrero, it is believed that masks assume the spirit of the animals they represent and protect the wearer against evil during religious ceremonies.

These masks are all from the first decades of the twentieth century and are from various states of Mexico. They represent a broad range of themes and technical skills.

art playing important roles in its evolution and growth. He personally shepherded it for almost fifty years, and upon his death in 1979, it became part of his estate. Rockefeller's daughter Ann purchased it from the estate in 1982; owing to her efforts the collection found permanent homes in two museums important for their rich cultural connections to Mexico—the San Antonio Museum of Art and the Mexican Museum in San Francisco.

The collection now numbers slightly more than three thousand objects, from all over Mexico and made from a wide variety of materials using many different techniques. Interestingly, the size of the collection has decreased over the years. In a letter dated July 6, 1942, Rockefeller writes, "In making a check I find that there are more than four thousand objects making up the list of folk or popular art from Mexico."[2] Apparently, many of the objects listed were purely decorative and purchased for use in recreating a Mexican market in the garden of the Museum of Modern Art in 1940. Some pieces disappeared; others, being ephemeral art, simply deteriorated. Still others were given away by Rockefeller to friends. Susan Herter, who worked with Rockefeller during his days as coordinator for Inter-American Affairs, said that "if you admired [an object], he would often give it to you."[3]

As is characteristic of most collections of Mexican folk art, ceramic objects make up more than fifty percent of the Rockefeller collection. The collection of textiles, consisting of more than two hundred pieces, is small but provides a fine overview of textiles made since the turn of the century, especially non-Indian textiles. Objects of corn husks, wood, straw, paper, shell, glass, tin, silver, wax and other materials constitute the remainder of the collection.

The majority of the pieces in the collection are by anonymous artists. Other works are by well-known personalities of the folk art world. The early part of the collection represents famous folk artists of the 1930s and 1940s, such as ceramists Doña Rosa of Oaxaca and Aurelio Flores of Izúcar de Matamoros, Puebla, and *popote* mosaic artist Felipe Olay of Mexico City. The part of the collection assembled after 1960 contains a large number of pieces by well-known modern folk artists: miniature—toy-maker Angel Carranza; ceramists Doña Teodora Blanco, Herón Martínez, the late Candelario

Medrano and the Aguilar family; internationally famous papier-mâché artist Pedro Linares; and others. In some instances, these pieces are signed by the artists, a custom that developed in response to commercial demand in the late 1960s.

In most cases, we know the provenance of objects. We also know something about the history of most objects after they left their places of origin. Some have impressive histories. The graceful lacquered gourd crane (pl. 125) from Olinalá, Guerrero, for example, first appeared in the 1930 *Mexican Arts* exhibition mounted by René d'Harnoncourt. In 1932 a picture of the crane was published in Frances Toor's magazine *Mexican Folkways* as part of an advertisement; presumably it was for sale at that time. Rockefeller possibly purchased the crane the following year, when he went to Mexico for the first time. It next appeared in public at the Museum of Modern Art in 1940, as part of the popular-art section of *20 Centuries of Mexican Art* but was not included in the catalogue. In 1969 it was shown again, this time as part of the exhibition of Rockefeller folk art at the Museum of Primitive Art. Several newspapers used a photograph of the by-then famous crane to illustrate their reviews of the exhibition. It was again displayed in 1984 as part of an exhibition at the Center for Inter-American Relations in New York and was prominently illustrated in the catalogue. When the Rockefeller collection was donated to the San Antonio Museum Association in 1985, the crane became a part of its permanent exhibition and is proudly displayed next to more recent lacquered pieces from Olinalá. Clearly, Rockefeller was very fond of the lacquered crane and thought that it was an important piece of folk art.

Another object with an impressive history of exhibition is the tin and glass frame containing nineteenth- and early-twentieth-century silver *milagros* (pl. 54). This assemblage was part of the Museo de Artes Populares exhibition in Mexico City mounted by Roberto Montenegro and Moisés Saenz in 1934, and a photograph of it was later published in a short catalogue. Many pieces in the exhibition were from Montenegro's private collection, which was taken to New York six years later for the Museum of Modern Art exhibition. A photograph of it was published in the catalogue of

Plate 3
Vendor's Display of *Milagros*.
Oaxaca, Oaxaca.
1978.
Cast metal, 15¾ X 12¼". SAMA.

This vendor's display of *milagros* shows how these small offerings typically are sold. A person has his choice of a multitude of *milagros* and is sore to find one corresponding to a miraculous recovery, cure or change in events he has recently experienced. The *milagro* is then hung by the grateful person inside the church near the saint who has effected the miraculous event. *Milagros* are small but significant tokens of gratitude. Contemporary *milagros* are made of cast metal and affixed to shiny ribbons.

Surely the man outside a Oaxaca church who sold his complete supply of *milagros* to Rockefeller in October 1978 must have bought himself a *milagro* in gratitude!

that show, and the assemblage presumably became a part of the Rockefeller collection after the exhibition was concluded. Its subsequent history parallels that of the crane: It is now a part of the permanent exhibition of Rockefeller materials in San Antonio.

The collection has not been previously described and analyzed in detail, but numerous publications on various aspects of it have appeared.[4] Various reviews of exhibitions of the collection through the years are also available and provide useful comments on its nature and significance.

Several aspects of the Rockefeller collection set it apart from similar collections and make it unique. Clearly, its sheer size and scope make it one of the most comprehensive groupings of Mexican folk art in the world. Its greatest importance, however, lies elsewhere. First, in a field in which any object of more than twenty-five years is likely to be labeled "old," the antiquity of many of the pieces is important. The early part of the collection, particularly that assembled by Rockefeller with the assistance of Roberto Montenegro, contains extremely rare and important pieces from the eighteenth and nineteenth centuries—objects unmatched in collections elsewhere. Splendid folk objects such as the eighteenth-century centurion helmet mask from the State of Mexico (pl. 56), the exquisitely painted lacquered dish from Michoacán (pl. 116), the expressive set of *conchero* pull toys (pl. 92), and many other historically significant objects are without parallel in other collections.

Second, Rockefeller's treasures are a result of fifty years of collecting activity. In several important instances the collection contains folk art from the same village purchased during the 1930s, the 1950s and the 1970s, allowing us a rare opportunity to identify patterns of continuity and change within a given area. Water-cooler supports from San Blas Atempa, Oaxaca, for example, span a century of production of this type of folk art in the Isthmus of Tehuantepec. The same chronological depth can be seen in dozens of other examples from the collection.

Finally, the collection—assembled by an unusually open-minded man with the assistance of artists, scholars, folk art connoisseurs and dealers—represents Mexican folk art over the past fifty years and, in some cases, longer.

THE NATURE OF THE COLLECTION

There are many ways of organizing the objects in a collection as rich and varied as this one is. Perhaps the most useful way of grouping them, however, is according to their function, since folk art is best understood through consideration of the context in which the objects are made and used. Four basic categories suggest themselves: utilitarian—objects made primarily for day-to-day use with specific duties in mind; ceremonial—pieces used only within a particular ritual context; recreational—objects associated with play, fantasy and entertainment; and decorative—objects created primarily for aesthetic reasons. These groupings are, admittedly, rough-hewn: while some objects fit into only one of the above categories, others might fit easily into two or three. For example, a painted clay skeleton with articulated limbs attached to a cord is ceremonial, because it was made to be used in Day of the Dead festivities. However, because the skeleton also functions as a toy, it might also be regarded as a recreational object. In what follows, an object's primary function will determine the category in which it is included.

UTILITARIAN OBJECTS

Today, as in the past, most Mexican folk art is primarily utilitarian. Carefully woven textiles used as clothing, cooking utensils, household furnishings and handmade containers of every shape and size are still found in abundance all over Mexico—particularly rural areas—even though plastics and machine-made clothing and objects are making steady inroads. All of these objects reflect and embody family or local traditions; each is uniquely designed to meet specific demands made by temperature, pattern of use, sex of wearer (in the case of clothing) and a variety of other factors. In short, the forms of these objects follow their functions.

The ceramics of Tulimán, Guerrero, a Nahua Indian community in the hills of southeastern Mexico, are primarily utilitarian. For hundreds of years, potters from this small community have produced highly prized three-handled water jugs used in dozens of villages in the region. What makes

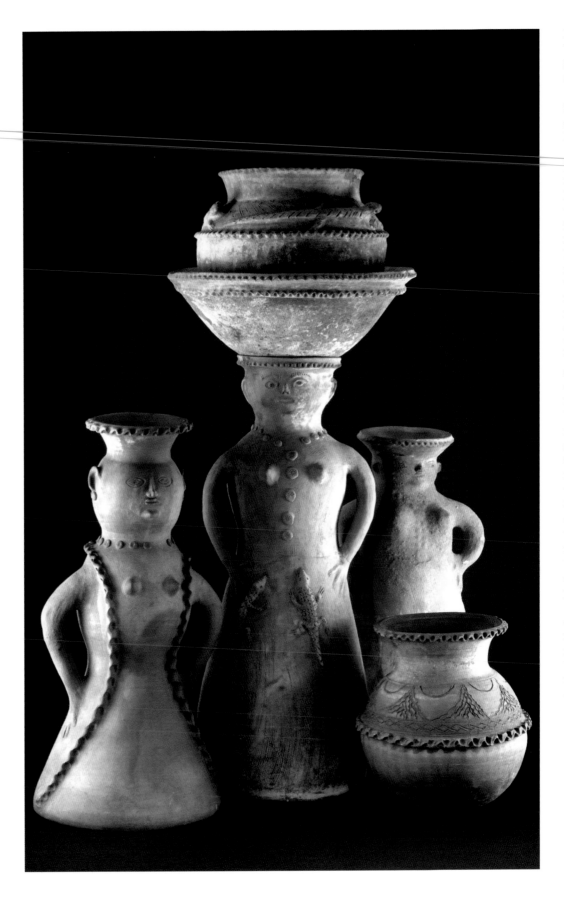

Plate 4
Water Coolers.
San Blas Atempa, Tehuantepec,
Oaxaca.
1940s to 1960s.
Single-fired earthenware,
approximately 29 X 14".
MM and SAMA.

Keeping water cool and fresh is critical in the hot Isthmus climate. San Blas Atempa water coolers have three parts. For this method of cooling, the base, a traditional female form, supports a shallow flared bowl that holds the water jar. Cooling is promoted through evaporation. These bases bear an abstract resemblance to the Tehuanas—the fabled women of Tehuantepec—whose distinctive and imposing physical presence is suggested by these solid and dignified ceramic sculptures. The three figures include a variety of surface treatments. A fluted band transforms a bare-breasted woman into a cloaked figure, and lizards crawl up the stomach toward a necklace that also serves as decorative buttons. The figure on the right is an unadorned version with little body contouring. Surface paint has long since peeled off these figures, bowls, and jars, which were acquired by Rockefeller from the garden of a Oaxaca family that had transformed them into containers for exotic semitropical plants.

Teodora Blanco, the great figural ceramist from Santa María Atzompa, was profoundly influenced not only by these forms but also by the highly stylized faces that bear resemblance to some pre-Hispanic ceramics.

Plate 5
Boot Pitchers.
Barrio de la Luz, Puebla.
1930s.
Painted and glazed earthenware,
11 X 9½ X 5". MM and SAMA.

Highly glazed, thick-walled boot
pitchers for pouring pulque were
mold-made by Barrio de la Luz
potters. These asymmetrical pitchers are amusing representations of
the high-heeled button-up shoes
worn by the women of nineteenth-
century Mexico.

these jugs attractive to the peasants who buy them is the ease with which
they can be used to transport water from distant village wells to individual
households and their suitability as storage containers. The lightness and
shape of the vessel, the curve of the handles and the size of the orifice all are
calculated to ease the gathering and carrying of the water. Furthermore, the
single-fired pottery of Tulimán is highly porous, so that the water remains
cool through evaporation. Because they must "sweat" constantly and freely,
these jugs have round bottoms to discourage their being placed on the
ground or on top of a table-settings that would impede cooling—and the
three handles allow them to be suspended from a pole or roof support. After
meeting such primary functional requirements, the potters of Tulimán are
free to embellish as they see fit. Two water jugs from Guerrero, one of them
from Tulimán (pl. 8), illustrate varying degrees to which these vessels are
decorated after the basic requirements have been met.

While utilitarian considerations are at the core of most Mexican folk art,
few artists are content to let their skills and imaginations rest at that level.
Roughly carved, squat stools are ingeniously transformed into armadillos,
horses and other animals. Strong, functional walking sticks become a tangle
of serpents and vines. This tendency of Mexican folk artists, and indeed folk
artists all over the world, not only to make, but also to create and to animate,
gives folk art its special quality and justifies its classification as art.

Ceramic Vessels

Among the objects whose function is mainly utilitarian, the most
impressive are perhaps the ceramics. These range from undecorated cooking
vessels from dozens of small Indian villages throughout Mexico to objects
that are embellished to a point that almost obscures their function.

The collection contains several splendid examples of highly burnished
black-ware made by the Zapotec potter Doña Rosa, of San Bartolo Coyotepec.
A large water jug (pl. 9) illustrates the sophistication of Doña Rosa's work and
the inherent strength of her plain but elegant ollas. It also demonstrates her

Plate 6
Pulque Pitcher.
Metepec, State of Mexico.
1940.
Mold-made and hand-formed
glazed earthenware, height, 16".
SAMA.

A leaping lizard attempting to partake of pulque became the innovative handle of this pulque pitcher.
Six cups that would have hung from
the protrusions beneath the neck
are sadly missing. The words "Recuerdo Feli[z] Año Nuevo" commemorate the New Year and help
establish a memory for the pur-
chaser. The exuberantly painted
pitcher is a mix of energetic brushstrokes and floral motifs. The lizard
takes us back to pre-Hispanic times,
when innovative potters ingeniously used animals for spouts, handles and relief decoration. The characteristic fine red Metepec clay
shows through the glaze of this
pulque jar.

Plate 7
Jar.
Tulimán, Guerrero.
1930s.
Single-fired earthenware with painted
slip design, 13 X 13". SAMA.

This large and graceful jar is designed for
storage. The symmetric floral motif is
painted with a natural slip made from local ore. The pieces are fired in large open
fires with the pottery piled up in the center of the flames.

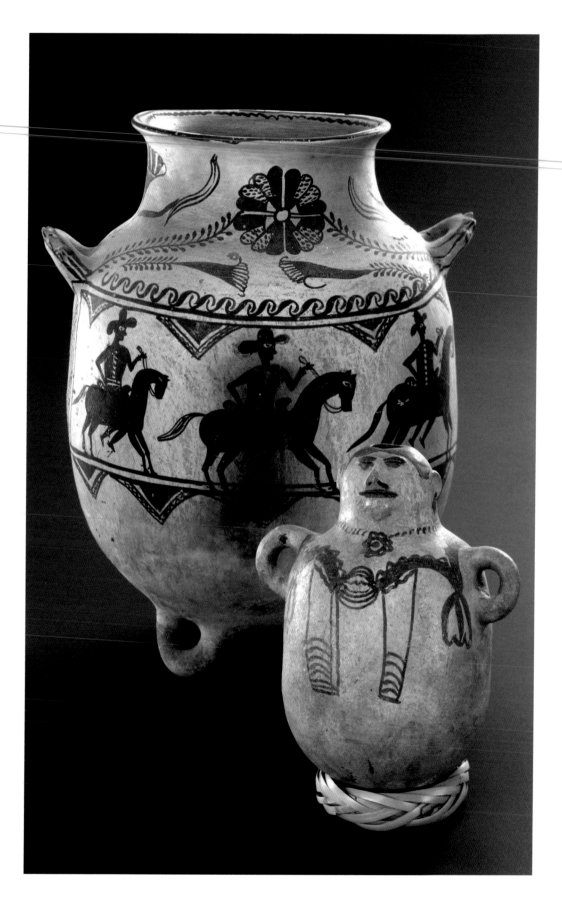

Plate 8
Water Jars.
Mezcala region, Guerrero;
Tulimán, Guerrero.
Left: Hand-molded, single-fired
ceramic with painted slip design,
18½ X 15"; right: hand-molded,
single-fired ceramic with painted
slip design; bamboo base;
9¾ X 7½". SAMA.

A Nahua Indian area in the State of
Guerrero known as the Mezcala region includes many pottery villages
still using pre-Hispanic ceramic
techniques. The artists of these villages have always produced a wide
variety of utilitarian pottery and in
recent years have produced new
and decorative pieces.

On the left, the large *cántaro*, designed for home water storage, is
made of a very porous clay that en-
hances cooling through surface
evaporation. The three legs that el-
evate the *cántaro* above the ground
assist with cooling. An almost identical piece was included in the Museum of Modern Art's 1940 exhibition, *20 Centuries of Mexican Art*.
The traditional design shows *charros* on western-type saddles. The
decorative painting style is always
free and confident, whether it consists of loose, repetitive geometric
motifs or profiled horsemen or animals. On the large *cántaro* the elegant horsemen face the viewer while
the horses' legs suggest a canter.

The smaller piece is an anthropomorphic canteen. Rope strung
through the handles makes it easy
to hang at home or carry back from
the river or stream.

Plate 9
Doña Rosa Real de Nieto.
Water Jar.
San Bartolo Coyotepec, Oaxaca.
1930s.
Burnished earthenware; bamboo
base; 15½ X 13½". SAMA.

This elegant black clay *cántaro* (water jar) epitomizes Doña Rosa's achievement as a folk artist. It is difficult to imagine how this small and fragile woman could hand-throw large and graceful jars on a primitive wheel. In her last years Doña Rosa became a living legend. Visitors and collectors from all over the world came to San Bartolo Coyotepec, a pottery center outside Oaxaca, to see her black clay pottery.

Black pottery is not black to begin with. At a critical point in firing, fuel is added to the fire, and the potter rapidly seals all openings to the kiln, producing thick smoke that impregnates the pieces with carbon. Before firing, the surfaces of the jars are burnished with a quartz burnishing stone. When the pieces are removed, they are polished with animal fat, wax or oil that seals them and produces a high luster. Doña Rosa's early pieces impressed, among others, Edward Weston, who photographed the classical shapes of her *cántaros.*

mastery of the coloration process achieved through reduction-firing, a technique in which carbon residue is bonded to clay in an airtight kiln. The handsome decoration of some Coyotepec earthenware is achieved through selective surface burnishing into geometric or floral designs prior to firing.

Other fine examples of purely utilitarian earthenware come from the State of Guerrero. Atzacoaloya, a small Nahua village outside the town of Chilapa, produces elegant *cántaros* that are highly regarded throughout the region for their shape, durability and effectiveness (pl. 10). Still other excellent examples of water vessels come from Zacualpa, Tulimán and Zumpango del Río, Guerrero. Another representative piece of utilitarian Guerrero pottery is a water jar (pl. 8) probably from San Agustín de las Flores, a Nahua village in the Mezcala region. This graceful jar was designed for water storage in the home. The highly porous clay and the three supports elevating the vessel above the floor permit maximum cooling. But, going well beyond these basic requirements, the creator of this jar painted a lively horizontal band of six horsemen, each of which has its own individual personality and design quality. Rockefeller purchased this piece in the 1960s, shortly after it was made, but it is strikingly similar to pieces from the same village made in the 1930s.[5]

Majolica pottery, a high-fired, glazed pottery introduced to Mexico by the Spanish in the sixteenth century, is a utilitarian ware strongly represented in the collection. Rare nineteenth-century plates and platters from Guanajuato (pl. 11) and Talavera-style objects from the same period in the city of Puebla are excellent examples of a type of Mexican pottery with strong Mediterranean roots.

Most of the early majolica in the Rockefeller collection is elaborately decorated with figural motifs and arabesque floral designs typical of this ceramic ware. Later examples in the collection, made in this century, also come from the states of Puebla and Guanajuato. The collection contains more than a dozen examples of majolica ware made by the well-known Guanajuato ceramist Gorky Gonzales, who was instrumental in the rebirth of early majolica designs in Guanajuato; his fine pieces are now marketed all over the world.

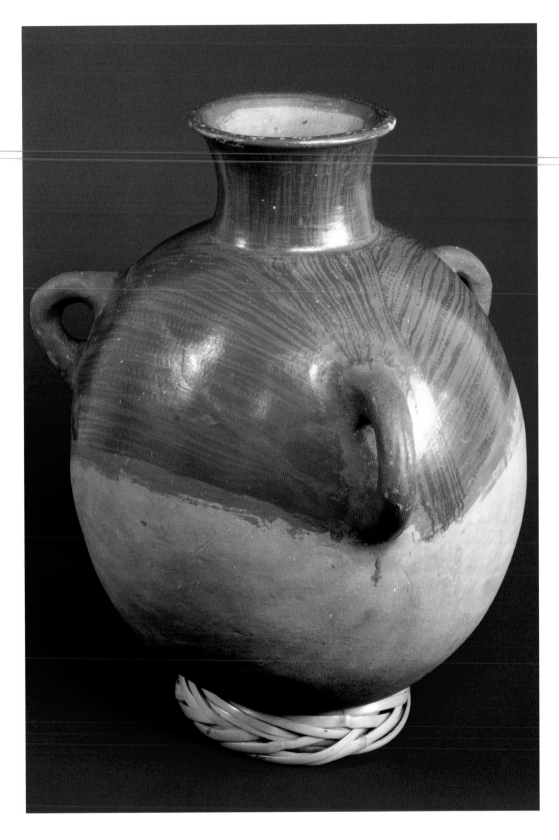

Plate 10
Water Jar.
Atzaeoaloya, Guerrero.
1930s.
Single-fired, burnished
earthenware; bamboo base;
14 X 12". SAMA.

This *cántaro*, from a Nahua village
near Chilapa, Guerrero, is a classic
example of utilitarian pottery. The
globular shape with three handles is
carried on burros, balanced on
heads and hung at home. It is made
of a porous buff-colored clay that al-
lows the evaporation necessary for
cooling. The bamboo ring elevates
the piece above the ground. Atzacoaloya produces other utilitarian
ware with similar surface decoration of roughly burnished sienna
slip on their upper surfaces. The
touch of the potter is felt not only in
the traditionally hand-built form
but also in the vigorous burnishing
strokes.

Plate 11
Platters.
Coroneo, Guanajuato.
Late 19th century.
Glazed and incised earthenware,
8½ X 6½". SAMA.

Folk artists often find an outlet for humor on serving platters. In these examples, amusing and primitive animals are incised in the clay and painted with a runny glaze. The effect is spontaneous and uninhibited. This very engaging utilitarian pottery seems to be a rural interpretation of the already-decadent majolica produced in nearby Dolores Hidalgo.

There are also many ceramic pitchers, primarily utilitarian but decorated in ways that are both beautiful and amusing. The exquisitely worked amber-colored pitcher (pl. 12) illustrates the delicate touch of some unknown nineteenth-century potter.[6] Portrait pitchers from the states of Michoacán, Mexico and Puebla were all used for the festive consumption of pulque.

Perhaps the most important utilitarian ceramic objects are the water cooler assemblages from San Blas Atempa, a Zapotec Indian community in the Isthmus of Tehuantepec. The collection has six fine examples. As mentioned earlier, one is from the nineteenth century, another from the 1940s and the rest are relatively modern, dating from the 1960s and 1970s. Each cooler set consists of three pieces—a figural base, a shallow bowl and an olla—which, together, maintain the freshness of a day's water supply. The cooler base in this piece (pl. 20) is extremely rare and may be the earliest surviving example of this folk art form anywhere.

Plate 12
Pitcher.
Oaxaca, Oaxaca.
19th century.
Glazed, hand-formed earthenware, 12¼ X 8". SAMA.

This charming pitcher is one of the rarest ceramic pieces in Rockefeller's collection. It was shown in the 1940 *20 Centuries of Mexican Art* exhibition at the Museum of Modern Art, with a caption that described it as a "type of ornamental jar unfortunately no longer made." The Spanish translation called it a rare sample of a lost art. The pitcher combines many stylistic techniques: press-molding, hand-forming, fluting, and relief work. It almost feels as if a potter and a baker collaborated to produce this very special piece.

Wooden Containers

About half of the fourteen wooden chests in the collection date from the nineteenth century, the rest from this century. Unquestionably, one of the most unusual is an elaborately carved chest (pl. 15) inlaid with woods of lighter hues. It is in superb condition. Unfortunately, little is known of its history, and its provenance is unknown. It is, however, typical of nineteenth- and early-twentieth-century inlaid furniture from the Mexican provinces, especially Oaxaca, Guerrero and Puebla, and reflects the strong Oriental influences found in much of the furniture of that period.[7]

Another important and quite interesting piece is a leather-covered wood chest (pl. 16). This shallow trunk is rare both for its shape and for the materials used in its manufacture. The hand-painted designs are a mixture of neoclassical architectural motifs associated with the early nineteenth century and floral designs. The iron hardware that secures the top, while suggestive of an earlier, perhaps colonial, period, is probably nineteenth-century, as is the iron key. Like the inlaid chest, it is an outstanding example of furniture

Plate 13
Pot.
Dolores Hidalgo, Guanajuato.
Late 19th century.
Glazed and painted majolica,
13 X 12". SAMA.

The tradition of Guanajuato majolica dates hack to the eighteenth
century. This type of majolica, similar to the Talavera ware of Puebla,
was brought to the newly wealthy,
silver-rich Guanajuato by the
Spaniards long after the Puebla potteries were established. In the nineteenth century, Padre Hidalgo, who
later became known as the father of
Mexican independence, encouraged
the Indians of Dolores to produce
the type of decorative wares being
made in nearby Guanajuato. He is
credited with the birth of Dolores
Hidalgo majolica. This hand-
thrown piece is glazed with traditional green, black, orange, sienna
and yellow over a creamy white
opaque background. Floral and bird
motifs are energetically painted in a
more free-flowing style than that of
Puebla.

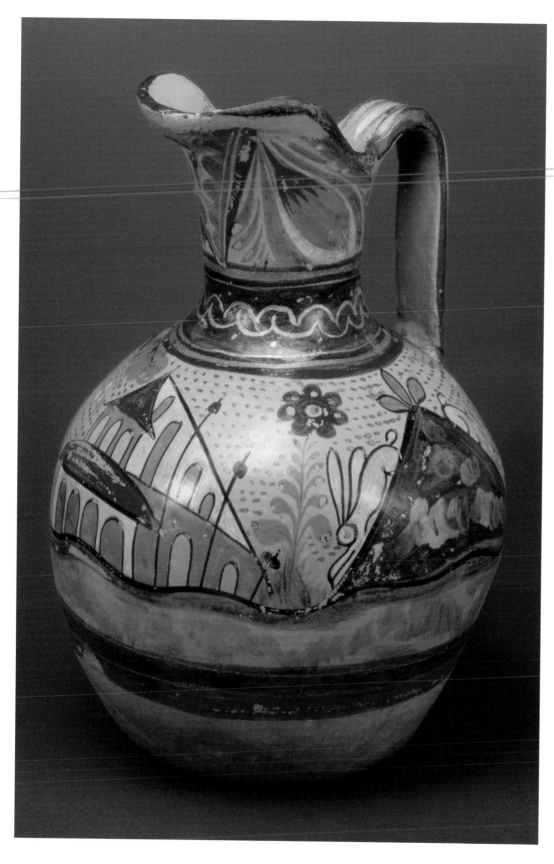

Plate 14
Pitcher.
Tonalá, Jalisco.
Late 19th century.
Single-fired earthenware and
metallic paint, height, 10". SAMA.

This late-nineteenth-century Tonalá
pitcher is probably one of the few
surviving pieces with painted gold
decoration. Pitchers from Tonalá
were used to keep water fresh and
cool, and the excellent clay often
imparted a fragrant taste and smell.
This mold-made piece is hand-
painted with what appears to be a
spontaneity of brushwork. Bound-
ing rabbits were popular animal
motifs, along with songbirds, birds
in flight and elaborate floral designs, and it was not unusual at that
time to paint images of village
chapels. These early pieces, once
painted, were given a coat of clear
varnish.

The palette used at the turn of
the century was somewhat different
than Tonaltecan color of today. All
the colors were natural pigments
mined locally. Today's combinations
are earthy colors with a dominant
light blue, pale green or cream
background. Rose, red and yellow
were once more fashionable. Much
like the ancient murals and wall
paintings, it is often hard to know
just how brilliant the original colors
were. They age gracefully and settle
into pastels of time and wear.

of the hinterland during the nineteenth century and early part of the twentieth. Its provenance, similarly, is unknown.

The largest selection of chests in the collection comes from Olinalá, Guerrero. Made from a highly fragrant *lináloe* wood, richly lacquered and painted, they manifest many of the finest folk qualities in Mexican painting and lacquer work (pls. 17, 18). Used primarily to store household linens and other valuables, these chests were greatly valued in rural Mexico as wedding gifts or as part of a dowry. Many were custom-made and dated, and they frequently included dedicatory verses.[8]

Olinalá chests are now shipped to all parts of Mexico and exported in great quantities to many places outside the republic. The collection contains several outstanding examples of these brightly colored chests. Most are richly painted on three sides and the top, inside and out. Street scenes from neighboring areas such as Izúcar de Matamoros and the city of Puebla are often included on the front panel (pls. 18, 24). The artists' concern for detail can be seen. Soldiers, flags, animals and other scenes of nineteenth-century life are depicted in a fanciful, yet straightforward, fashion. Nationalistic emblems, most frequently the Mexican eagle atop a cactus and flags, are often part of the design motifs of trunks from Olinalá.

Other lacquered chests in the collection come from Michoacán and are richly decorated in a manner distinct from those of Olinalá.

Also in the collection is a large and impressive assortment of lacquered plates and bowls and trays, mainly from Michoacán. Here, again, the variously shaped objects, decorated with floral motifs typical of the nineteenth century, show an Oriental influence. Trays from Uruapan (pl. 28), decorated using an inlaid lacquer technique, are interesting for comparison with the other pieces.

Textiles

The collection has more than 150 textiles, the majority of which are from the twentieth century. With few exceptions, they are in excellent condition.

Plate 15
Chest.
Possibly from Olinalá, Guerrero.
Early 1920s.
Inlaid wood and metal,
32 X 14 X 17½". SAMA.

This inlaid wooden chest is reminiscent of nineteenth-century work. In fact it was probably commissioned in 1933 as a present for Nelson's father, John D. Rockefeller, Jr., as evidenced by the initials "JR" on the front of the chest. Since Nelson Rockefeller never visited the remote Guerrero village of Olinalá, it is likely that Frances Flynn Paine, a great champion of Olinalá lacquerware, commissioned this piece. These dowry chests can be found in many Olinalá households but are rarely made for external markets. The inlaid floral designs are very similar to delicate painted motifs found on lacquered chests. Elements of traditional work are also seen in the geometric border designs that set off the inlaid work on the body of the chest.

Plate 16
Trunk.
19th century.
Painted leather on wood,
29 X 16 X 10". SAMA.

Although the exact origin of this unusual leather-covered trunk is difficult to determine, it might have been found in a rural hacienda near Puebla because of its curious mixture of motifs: the popular floral designs seen on Talavera-style pottery from Puebla and neoclassical pillars from *portales*—those wonderful covered walkways that surround a town's central plaza. The use of ornate wrought-iron hardware shows a definite Spanish influence. The Spaniards brought wrought iron to Mexico; after the Conquest blacksmith guilds were divided into locksmiths and bladesmiths. Puebla and Amozoc were centers for most of the elaborate ironwork in Mexico. Leather-covered trunks were popular in colonial Mexico but are rarely seen today.

Plate 17
Chest.
Olinalá, Guerrero.
Late 19th century.
Lacquered and painted wood,
12 X 29 X 15½". SAMA.

Lacquerware is one of Mexico's oldest crafts, and evidence of widespread pre-Hispanic Indian production is conclusive. When the Spaniards arrived in Mexico, they were stunned by the brilliant and diverse selection of lacquerware they saw in the Aztec marketplaces. Olinalá, a small village in the rugged Sierra Madre del Sur of Guerrero, was and still is devoted to this labor-intensive craft. The techniques of lacquerware have not changed significantly for hundreds of years.

The base material for Olinalá lacquer is chia oil extracted from the crushed and boiled chia seeds. After the first coat of oil and powdered dolomite is applied and burnished with the heel of the hand, layers of the oil and locally mined pigments are applied and polished, building up a very resistant base. This lacquered base can then be decorated with paints that nineteenth-century artisans made with natural pigments. The traditional base colors are a deep orange-red or black. Two techniques are now practiced in Olinalá, *rayado* (incised) and *dorado* (painted).

Rockefeller's collection of lacquered chests is a testimony to the splendid colonial and late-nineteenth-century work produced in Olinalá. René d'Harnoncourt and Fred Davis helped re-vive this craft in the late 1920s, and the late Carlos Espejel was instrumental in reviving it once again in the late 1960s, when the number of artisans had dwindled to seven. Lacquerware is now produced in most Olinalá households.

Today lacquerware is a communal craft involving many artisans who are specialists in the many techniques necessary to complete a piece. Five or more artisans work on one painted dowry chest. A carpenter makes the wooden chest from the highly fragrant *lináloe* wood harvested in the tropical areas of Guerrero. Various family members collect the minerals and make the oil and pigments. A woman generally performs the critical burnishing of the base coat. Polishing is performed by a specialist, and a painter completes the work.

This extraordinary dowry chest is one of the earliest pieces of lacquerware in the Rockefeller collection. An abundance of large, loosely painted flowers and foliage surrounds mounted horsemen and figures on a rich burnt-orange lacquered background. The panels are framed with simple bands of colors unlike the patterned border designs seen on other Olinalá chests. Time has faded the once-brilliant pigments to subtle autumnal hues. The painter of this trunk skillfully integrated the figures, animals and floral motifs into a structured yet freely executed design.

Plate 18
Chest.
Olinalá, Guerrero.
Late 19th century.
Lacquered and painted wood,
13⅞ X 28 X 13¾". MM.

This dowry chest is typical of the nineteenth-century style of pictorial decoration popular in Olinalá. Although the village was in a remote part of the Sierra Madre del Sur, the artisans took pleasure in copying urban scenes they found in books. The curious painting on the front panel combines cathedrals and colonial buildings against a backdrop of mountains. The charming confusion of perspectives is very common on these lacquered chests. The top of the trunk is decorated with the ever-popular patriotic motif of the eagle, cactus and serpent surrounded by Mexican flags. Pelicans, cranes, flowers and a variety of border designs complete this very traditional chest. The background color is a rich burnt orange.

Most are mestizo textiles, produced on Spanish-style looms in weaving centers such as Chiconcuac, State of Mexico; Santa Ana Chiautempan, Tlaxcala; and Teotitlán del Valle, Oaxaca. Less numerous but of no less importance are the Indian textiles, most of which were produced on back-strap looms. *Huipiles, quechquémitls, fajas, bolsas* and other items from Indian Mexico provide an interesting contrast to the large collection of non-Indian materials.

In general, the quality of Mexican textiles has declined sharply since the 1950s. By and large, later textiles reflect an increasing lack of attention to tightness of weave, consistency of dyeing, intricacy of embroidery and other measures of excellence. Most of the textiles in the Rockefeller collection come from an earlier period, when a high standard was maintained.

The collection contains many fine examples of the tightly woven wool sarapes made during the first quarter of this century for *charros*.[9] Made on Spanish-style looms—as opposed to the back-strap loom, which predates the Spanish conquest—these sarapes are usually composed of solid or repeating motif fields, decorated with traditional geometric designs, such as stepped-

Plate 19
Fiesta Huipil.
Huatla de Jiménez, Oaxaca.
1920s.
Hand-loomed cotton, silk,
ribbons, and lace, 36 X 25".
SAMA.

This classic fiesta *huipil* from the mountainous Mazatec region of Oaxaca is worn for ceremonial occasions. There is a striking contrast between the carefully woven open-meshed strips and the wildly exuberant silk ribbons that join them. The central panel is embroidered with a stylized parrot and a hummingbird partaking of floral nectar. Floral bands circle the bottom of the *huipil* and help to reinforce the weave at the shoulders. Imported silk threads are used for embroidering.

The *huipil*, a woman's tuniclike costume, was called *huipili* by the Aztecs. It is the most commonly worn garment in Indian Mexico. It is made by joining rectangular strips woven on a back-strap loom. The weave can vary from gauze-like fabric to tightly woven cotton. The surface can be adorned with intricate or simple embroidery in geometric or floral and animal motifs. The embroidery stitches include a great variety of techniques, from simple cross-stitch to elaborate brocading. These loose-fitting garments are made for everyday use and for ceremonial occasions. A finely woven *huipil* is expected to last a lifetime and often is a symbol of status for the weaver.

Plate 20
Water Cooler.
San Blas Atempa, Tehuantepec,
Oaxaca.
Late 19th century.
Painted, single-fired earthenware,
36 X 16". SAMA.

This classic late-nineteenth-century
tinajera (water cooler) is one of the
most important pieces in the collection. The three-part set is missing
the shallow bowl that ordinarily sits
on top of the figure and holds the
jar of drinking water. Water is
cooled through the process of evaporation, made possible by the
highly porous clay the piece is made
of. The flared bowl, placed between
the figure and the *cántaro*, is filled
with sand to absorb excess moisture
and promote further cooling. These
pieces are a sculptural translation of
the traditional water-carrying pos-
ture.

   These anthropomorphic figures
are traditionally women, but this
unusual piece appears to be a male
with a black beard and stylized
mustache. A pendant adorns his
neck, and his torso is decorated
with a floral motif. The water jar is
very coarse clay with a fluted coil
circling the piece. A floral design
incised on the upper part of the jar
is similar to pre-Conquest decoration.

Plates 21 and 22
Saddle and Detail.
Amozoc, Puebla.
Early 20th century.
Leather, silver, metal and bone,
40 X 29 X 20". SAMA.

The art of saddlery was taken very seriously in Mexico, where not only transportation but entertainment for wealthy Mexicans revolved around horses. Horseback riding, introduced by the Spaniards, is considered a national sport in Mexico. Shortly after the Conquest, the Mexicans were forbidden to ride by the Spaniards, who set themselves apart by lavish displays on horseback, including processions, promenades and competitions. But the inevitable occurred on provincial ranches, where successful Mexican landholders bought horses and took up riding. They dressed in elaborate costumes adorned with silver and embroidery and outfitted their horses similarly. They were called *charros*, meaning "loud and flashy."

This saddle would have been used by a *charro* in a parade on a national holiday or in a *charreada*, where all kinds of equestrian events take place. It is made of carved and appliquéd leather with elaborate leather roses. The metalwork of engraved and encrusted steel is a traditional craft in Amozoc, Puebla, where artisans make elaborate spurs, bits and decorative accessories for *charros*. The whole effect is one of opulence, a carryover from the sixteenth century, when class divisions were intensified by this sport's lavish manifestations.

Plate 23
Chest (front panel).
Quiroga, Michoacán.
19th century.
Lacquered wood,
16¼ X 30½ X 14½". SAMA.

This nineteenth-century chest documents the elegant costumes of high-ranking military officers in Mexico's struggle for independence from Spain. These splendid uniforms, inspired by European military fashion, were decidedly French, with occasional Spanish influence. Paintings of Mexico's fight for independence show Agustín de Iturbide, General Antonio López de Santa Anna and other important officers impeccably dressed in white breeches with tiny gold buttons, red and white tight-waisted short jackets elegantly trimmed with gold epaulets and braiding and gold-tasseled cummerbunds. Hats were copies of a French military style. Rifles and bayonets were often skillfully engraved. The border designs and floral motifs around the soldiers are classic Uruapan patterns used on Michoacán lacquerware.

Plates 24 and 25
Chest and Detail.
Olinalá, Guerrero.
Late 19th century.
Lacquered and painted wood,
16½ X 30 X 16". SAMA.

This classic Olinalá piece was intended to be a dowry chest. Many colonial chests had panels painted with charming and idealized scenes of rural and urban life, such as those depicted here. The more sophisticated urban scenes were copied from books and have a distinctly naive quality. The border designs are a mix of geometric and floral motifs. The front panels are colonial scenes of the city of Puebla or Cholula with their magnificent central squares, imposing stone buildings and impressive churches. The side panels are pastoral scenes located in and around Olinalá with vistas of the surrounding mountains. The side panels of the lid are decorated with cranes—popular with Olinalátecos.

Plate 26
Chest.
Olinalá, Guerrero.
Late 19th century.
Lacquered and painted wood,
14¾ X 33 X 16⅝". SAMA.

This chest has a traditional deep orange-red lacquered base painted with a profusion of floral, animal and architectural motifs. A colonial panorama is set behind a grassy courtyard filled with a menagerie of rabbits, docks, cranes, pelicans and dogs. They are larger than the trees. The lid is painted with the ancient eagle-and-serpent motif surrounded by Mexican flags. Nineteenth-century dowry chests were painted a solid color on the inside. It is common to find the initials of the young woman for whom the chest was made on the inside of the lid, surrounded by decorative motifs.

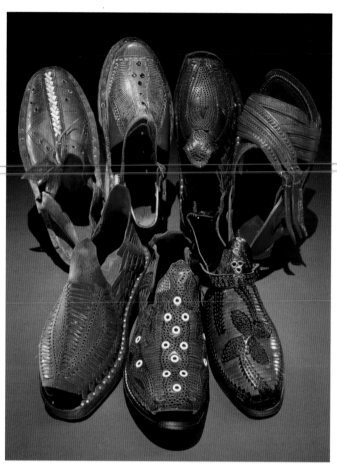

Plate 27
Huaraches.
States of Jalisco, Michoacán and Oaxaca.
1930 to 1960s.
Leather, grommets, nails and rubber tire treads, 10½ X 3½" to 11¾ X 4⅜". MM and SAMA.

Huaraches are the footwear of Indian Mexico. They are traditionally worn by men—Indian women in the past usually went barefoot. They have been worn in Mexico since pre-Hispanic times and are well-documented in all the early codices. Stylistic variations appear from state to state and developed according to terrain and climate. Huaraches are almost always made of leather. The soles were once made of laminated leather but are now made of rubber automobile tire treads. Huaraches can be laced, lashed, buckled on or just slipped into.

Plate 28
Tray.
Uruapan, Michoacán.
Early 20th century.
Encrusted lacquerware and wood, diameter, 22½". SAMA.

This early-twentieth-century *batea* (tray) is typical of the traditional *embutido* (encrusted) technique of lacquerware practiced in Uruapan since organized guilds were set up in the sixteenth century under the direction of Don Vasco de Quiroga, who introduced this elegant craft to the Tarascans in Uruapan, Periban and Quiroga.

Many steps are involved in making this tray. After the first coat of lacquer is hardened, the design is incised with a very sharp metal tool and hollowed out. These hollowed areas are filled with lacquer—colored mineral powders mixed with the fat extracted from boiling *aje* insects—and rubbed vigorously with the palm of the hand to achieve a high luster. Many colors can be used on one tray for the inlaid design. In the old days the colors were natural pigments mined in the area. Recipes for these colors were passed down for generations within families. The early pieces had a refined delicacy and austere symmetry that have given way to profuse decoration. This *batea* has delicate floral motifs surrounding two stylized figures and their animals. The geometric border design is a classic Uruapan design used on gourds and trays.

Plate 29
Sarape (detail).
Saltillo, Coahuila.
Early 20th century.
Wool, cotton and aniline dyes,
45 X 88" (full size). SAMA.

This detail is of the central section
of a "portrait" sarape in vogue in
the late nineteenth and early twentieth century in Zacatecas and
Saltillo. In the midst of the striking
and complex triangular patterning
are two mustached *charros*, one
toasting the other with his glass of
tequila and the other raising a knife.
Are they engaged in a drinking bout
or toasting an occasion? These sarapes were often commemorative, the
central motifs portraying political
heroes, national symbols and popular themes. The shredded areas of
the sarape reveal the underlying
white cotton warp threads.

Plates 30, 31, 32
Sarapes (details).
Top to bottom: San Bernardino
Contla, Tlaxcala; Texcoco, State of
Mexico; Santa Ana Chiautempan,
Tlaxcala.
1930s.
Wool, 6'4" X 4'5" to 7 X 5' (full
size). MM and SAMA.

In pre-Hispanic times, Indians wore
a capelike garment similar to a sarape
but woven of cotton or other plant
fibers. Upright treadle hand looms
were introduced to Mexico by the
Spaniards, who also taught the Indians how to gather and spin wool,
profoundly influencing the development of the sarape.

A sarape, generally the size of a
blanket, is usually made of wool and
can be woven in one or two pieces.
As an all-purpose part of a man's
costume, it can be folded and worn
decoratively across his shoulders or
worn as a cloak. It can also be used
as a blanket or as a ground cover
for displaying market wares. Many
sarapes have a slit in the center so
they can be slipped over the head,
becoming useful for riding, rainy
weather or walking. Mexican weaving centers are identified by their
sarape designs. Rockefeller, particularly fond of sarapes from San
Bernardino Contla, Tlaxcala, continued to collect sarapes into the late
1970s.

The central design seen in the detail at top is a variation on the traditional diamond pattern—a broken
diamond combining geometric motifs. The warp is cotton and the weft
naturally dyed indigo. The center detail depicts a central design of zigzags
surrounded by floral and abstract
bird motifs. The bright colors are re-
peated in the border designs and as
background accents. The exciting
optical pattern in the detail at bottom
is a variation on the serrated diamond motif, surrounded by serrated
hourglass shapes. Diamonds within
diamonds were used in traditional
Tlaxcala and Saltillo sarape designs.
Another traditional motif, the
chevron, is used as an overall accent
and on the borders. Aniline dyes are
responsible for the vivid colors.

Plates 33 and 34
Rebozos.
Santa María del Río, San Luis
Potosí.
Late 19th century.
Silk, cotton, natural dyes and
gold thread, approximately
97 X 33" (full size).
MM and SAMA.

A rebozo is an indispensable part
of the mestiza and Indian
woman's wardrobe. It serves as a
shawl, a baby carrier, a head covering, a support for a basket or
cántaro and is used in certain indigenous dances. It can be intricately woven in complex *ikat* patterns or coarsely woven in cotton
or wool. In the eighteenth cen-

the surface with rural scenes. Rebozos were originally woven for
mestiza women who would not
dress like the Indians and yet
could not afford Spanish finery.
They have since been adopted by
Indians.

The rebozos in Rockefeller's
collection come from Santa María
del Río and Tenancingo, where
the finest rebozos in Mexico were
woven on back-strap and upright
looms. These rebozos can easily
take over a month to make, since
the process involves complex tie-
dyeing and loom setup. The
weaving takes at least two weeks,
and the elaborate fringe must be
finger-knotted into complex patterns learned when the artisans

In the detail on the left, one
can see this rebozo's lacy, web-
like pattern, called *granizo* (web
or cloud over the eyes). On the
right is a detail of a particularly
beautiful rebozo that combines
naturally dyed yellow silk with
gold threads. The method used
to make the delicate fringe dates
back to the early eighteenth century. The fringes of Rockefeller's
rebozos all have different patterns. Each of these fine silk rebozos weighs approximately ¾
pound and often has over 7,000
weft threads. The very finest rebozo can be pulled through a
wedding ring. The silk threads
traditionally were dyed with
plants, nuts and insect dyes. The

left comes from cochineal, a dye
made from cactus parasites.

Deciphering the various
threads of the rebozo's history is
complex. The multitude of influences was global—Chinese silk
and scarves, Southeast Asian *ikat*
shawls that arrived with the
Manila galleon, pre-Hispanic woven garments and Spanish and
Moorish designs. The blend o
cultures in this traditional Mexi
can shawl is as varied as its uses

Plate 35
Rebozo Fringe.
Michoacán.
1930s.
Cotton and synthetic silk, width, 9".
SAMA.

Elaborate fringes are the glorious finales of rebozos. Threaded in purple into this layered fringe of dyed synthetic silk is the name Uruapan, a principal city in the Tarascan sierra. The fringe is reminiscent of the fine-feathered lower edge of the unique tuniclike costumes worn by the ancient Tarascan warriors. At the time of the Spanish Conquest, the craftsmen of this region were well known for their luxurious featherwork, illustrated in the *Relación de Michoacán*, a sixteenth-century book by Spanish missionaries. The tightly woven black and indigo-blue fabric is still made in the sierra of Michoacán, where different villages each have individually and imperceptibly modified this traditional style.

Plate 36
Feliciana Martínez.
Embroidered Sampler.
Central Mexico.
Late 19th century.
Cotton and silk; tin frame;
26 X 18". SAMA.

Mexican samplers are a compendium of stitchery and popular embroidered designs. They differ from the traditional American samplers that incorporate a poem or text. The Spaniards brought many of their skills to Mexico after the Conquest, and their traditions, mixed with centuries of Moorish occupation, created a wealth of craft techniques easily transmitted to the highly skilled and artistic indigenous population. Young Mexican girls in convents were trained by devout Spanish nuns, who taught them all they knew about stitches, fabric making and design. These highly skilled girls went on to adorn *servilletas,* altar cloths and clothing for clerics and the wealthy, whose finery reflected their status.

This large sampler includes crossstitch, herringbone, satin stitch, reverse satin stitch, fish bone, stem and feather stitch. This piece is relatively elementary—there is no drawn or gauze work. Samplers are always signed and usually dated. This sampler, made by a seven- or eight-year-old, reads "Lo iso Felisiana Martines." It should have read "Lo hizo Feliciana Martínez" ("Made by Feliciana Martínez").

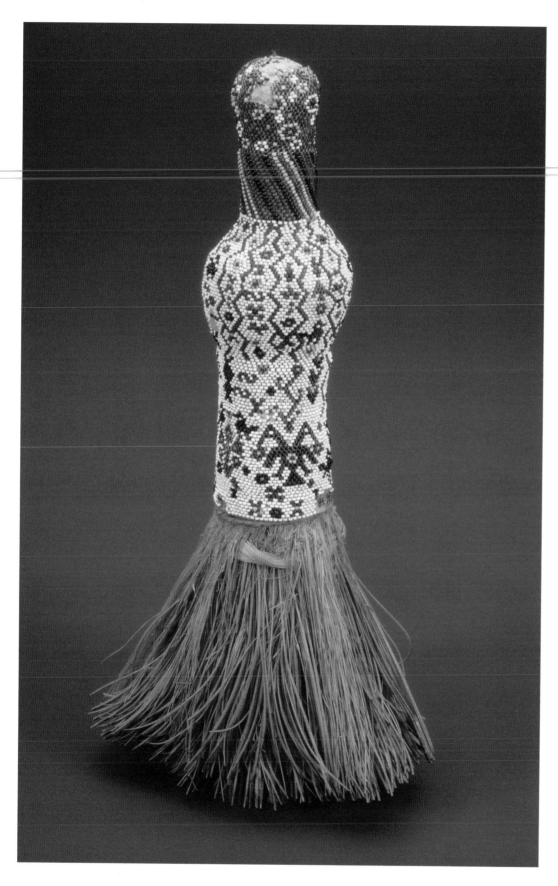

Plate 37
Rebozo Whisk Broom.
19th century.
Broomstraw and beads, 8¼ X 1¼".
SAMA.

When rebozos had elaborate silk fringes it was often necessary to comb out and unsnarl the tangles that developed in storage or in use or after washing. Each woman had a small broom used to straighten out the thousands of threads left after the fringe has been designed and macraméd. There is an old proverb to the effect that a woman's beauty is judged "by her braids and by her rebozo."

This nineteenth-century whisk broom has been gathered at the top with delicate beading in a combination of floral and geometric patterns and the ever-present double headed eagle. It was probably bought along with the many exquisite silk rebozos Rockefeller collected.

Plate 38
Uriarte family.
Talavera Jar.
Puebla, Puebla.
Late 19th century.
Painted and glazed earthenware,
19 X 12". SAMA.

Talavera poblana is the Mexican variation of Spanish majolica ware produced in Talavera de la Reina and other Spanish cities. Spanish majolica was derived from Italian Renaissance majolica, with Moorish, Islamic and Far Eastern influences. The craft was brought to Mexico immediately following the Conquest when the Spanish settled the city of Puebla. This very beautiful glazed pottery was originally produced in Puebla only by Spanish artisans under strict guild control. Glazing had been unknown in pre-Hispanic Mexico. The stylish pottery was produced in great quantities by well-organized potteries to meet the need for tableware, architectural tiles and utilitarian pottery in the New World. Today only a few workshops exist that make this elegant cobalt blue and white pottery according to the original Spanish method. Talavera pottery was enormously popular in colonial Mexico. Over seventy-five potteries were still at work in 1890. A century later there are only five.

Blended clays are mixed and prepared according to strict formulas. The rich opaque undercoat glaze is a perfect base for the thick cobalt oxide (blue) outer glaze. The long firings give these pieces their brilliant surface. This large, lidded jar combines traditional decorative motifs and stylized floral arrangements on an Oriental form. It was made in the Uriarte ceramic factory, one of the oldest family potteries in Puebla.

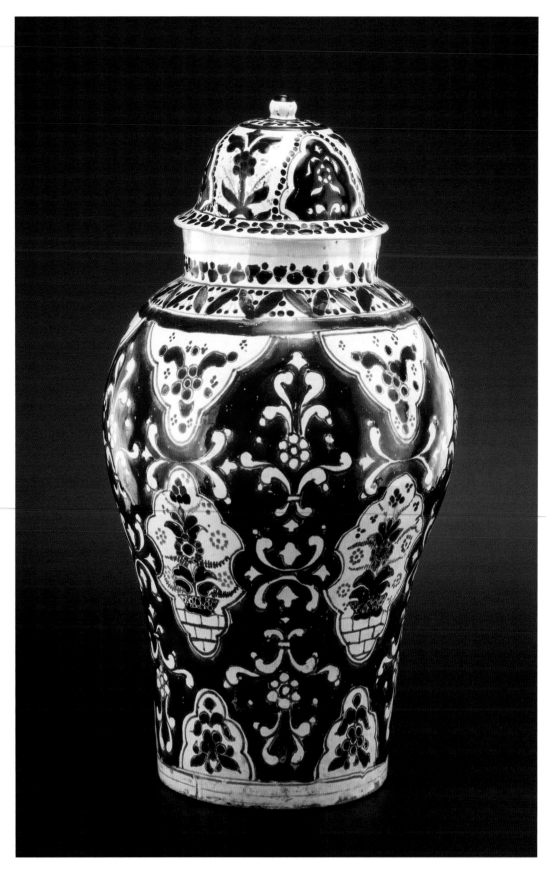

Plate 39
Portrait Pitchers.
Metepec, State of Mexico; Santa Fe de la Laguna and Quiroga, Michoacán.
Late 19th century to 1930s.
Single-fired, glazed and painted earthenware, 6" to 13¼".
MM and SAMA.

Portrait pitchers have a long history in Mexico, where commemorative and patriotic ceramics were popular in the mid-nineteenth century. Just as the gourd is a natural container, heads and torsos suggest a variety of pitcher forms fulfilling different purposes. The two pitchers in the foreground are made in similar molds but painted and glazed for different effects.

The late-nineteenth-century pulque pitcher in the center of the photograph is hauntingly and delicately painted. Some of these pitchers combine hand-thrown forms with press-molded features.

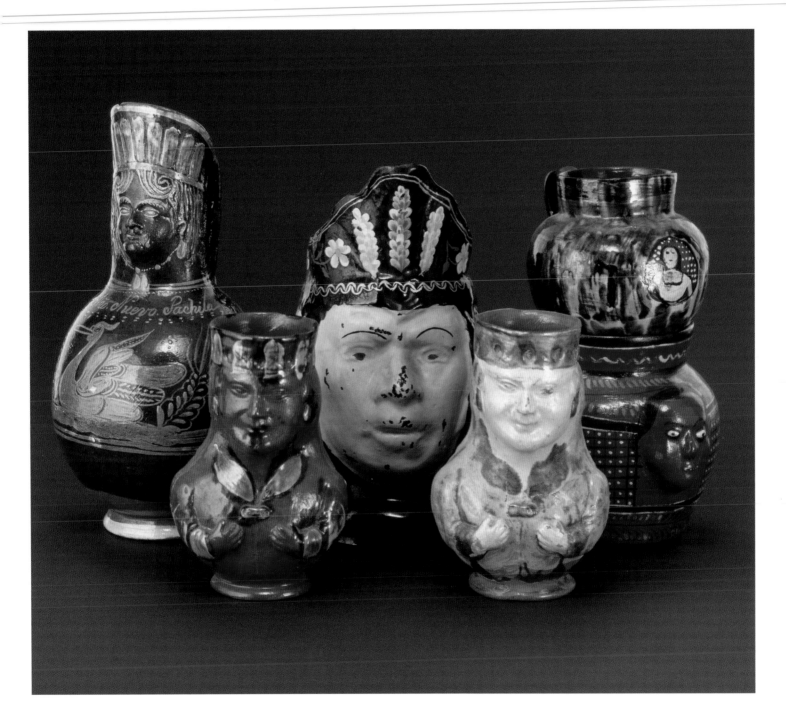

Plate 40
Mescal Container.
San Bartolo Coyotepec, Oaxaca.
1930s.
Black pottery, 10 X 4½". SAMA.

This very wide-eyed monkey, holding a small jar that says "Salero"
(saltcellar), is a container for
mescal, a potent alcoholic drink
made from the maguey plant. The
jar is for holding the salt that is often eaten as an accompaniment to
drinking mescal. Perhaps this
piece's monkey form implies that
after one drink you start to act like
an energetic monkey, losing some
inhibitions and careening about.
Oaxaca is famous for its mescal, and
these monkeys are filled, often
painted and then wrapped in a sisal
net as a holder—a perfect souvenir
to carry away from Oaxaca!

Many of these monkeys are
mold-made and hand-finished, giving each one an individual expression. Mexicans favor ancient symbols, and the monkey has been one
of their favorite animal motifs since
pre-Conquest times.

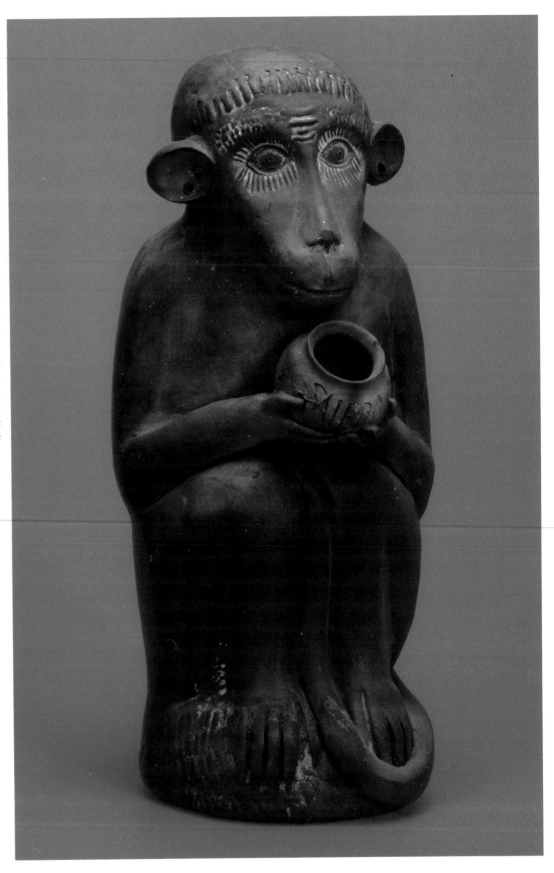

fret motifs. Technically, they are of very high quality and compare favorably with superior twentieth-century sarapes in other collections.

A sarape from northern Mexico, possibly Saltillo or Zacatecas, was acquired by Rockefeller in the 1930s. Although it has suffered insect damage, it is an excellent example of the degree to which textiles are sometimes embellished. The multicolored field is woven in a complicated diamond triangular pattern. The medallion in the center (pl. 29) shows two men dressed in clothing typical of rural Mexico in the early twentieth century. What is going on between them is not entirely clear, but they appear to be engaged in a drinking bout. While the content of this medallion is unusual, the use of decorated center medallions in Mexican sarapes goes back to the eighteenth century in Saltillo. It is still found in Zacatecas and other weaving centers of northern Mexico, where center sections often contain portraits of political leaders and famous figures from Mexican history.[10]

The collection contains an exceptionally fine selection of rebozos, mainly from Santa María del Río, San Luis Potosí and Tenancingo, State of Mexico. The rebozo, once an essential element of rural and urban dress, especially for the lower classes, was among the most utilitarian of textiles. Today, it is still used by peasant women to keep warm, to haul wood, to carry and clean infants, to block the hot rays of the Mexican sun, to preserve the warmth of tortillas, to cushion against a hard stone bench and to drape themselves with while attending Catholic Mass. Rebozos are wrapped, tied and hung in dozens of different ways, each a special response to the particular situation at hand. Rebozos for everyday use, some richly dyed and woven using the traditional *ikat* method, are represented in the greatest number. The truly important rebozos, however, are those that were meant to be worn on special occasions by the well-to-do. A rare, early-twentieth-century rebozo from Santa María del Río was acquired by Rockefeller in the 1930s. This silk rebozo (pl. 34) contains threads of gold interwoven with bands of *ikat*-dyed designs. The elaborately knotted fringe is reminiscent of the fringes of elegant rebozos from the eighteenth century.[11]

Of the Indian textiles in the collection, two *huipiles* from the Mazatec region of the State of Oaxaca are among the most important. One was worn

Plate 41
Bed Cover (detail).
Huixquilulcan, State of Mexico.
Early 20th century.
Hand-loomed wool,
8' X 6'4" (full size). SAMA.

This hand-loomed embroidery is covered with a profusion of cross- and satin-stitch animals, flowers, birds and deer, with a dominant tree-of-life motif. The tight cross-stitch creates a raised surface design. Many of the embroidery motifs are similar to the popular designs seen on eighteenth- and nineteenth-century samplers and have been part of Mexico's design vocabulary for hundreds of years. Floral and bird motifs, which are thought of as purely decorative, often had symbolic meaning in the past. The tree of life is a popular design throughout Puebla and is often incorporated into Otomí and Nahua embroideries.

by a child, the other (pl. 19) by an adult from the village of Huatla de Jiménez, an isolated community renowned for its ritual use of hallucinogenic mushrooms. Both are outstanding examples of Indian weaving and embroidery characteristic of festive dress during the first half of this century.

Another exquisite textile from Indian Mexico is a beaded blouse (pl. 43) from the Sierra de Puebla, acquired during the 1930s. Blouses, introduced from Europe, have replaced *huipiles* in many Indian villages in Mexico but often continue to exhibit old traditional design motifs. Today, in the State of Puebla, Nahua and Otomi Indians wear them on special occasions. This example is noteworthy because of its rarity, fine condition and exceptional quality.

Quechquémitls from the Huastec region of Mexico and other areas, *fajas* from Oaxaca, Michoacán, the State of Mexico and intricately woven Huichol and Otomí *morrales* from the states of Nayarit and Hidalgo, respectively, comprise the rest of the Indian portion of the textile collection.

In summary, the textile portion of the Rockefeller collection of utilitarian objects is small but of consistently high quality. The sarapes, *huipiles*, rebozos and other objects collected during the 1930s are rarely found in museum collections today.

CEREMONIAL OBJECTS

The most dramatic objects in the Rockefeller collection are those associated with ceremony, primarily religious. Such works of art, intended for use in ritual and celebration, embody and proclaim the energetic spirit that infuses much of the folk art of Mexico. Through these pieces, Mexicans are able to commune with the saints, maintain continuity between the living and the dead and strengthen the ties of family, community and nation.

Every day of the year, somewhere in Mexico, ceremonial folk art is being used in ways prescribed by local tradition to celebrate religious or secular events. During certain times of the Catholic calendar—Holy Week, the Day of the Dead and Christmas—the celebrations are particularly intense, involving the entire community, as well as the artists and artisans who produce

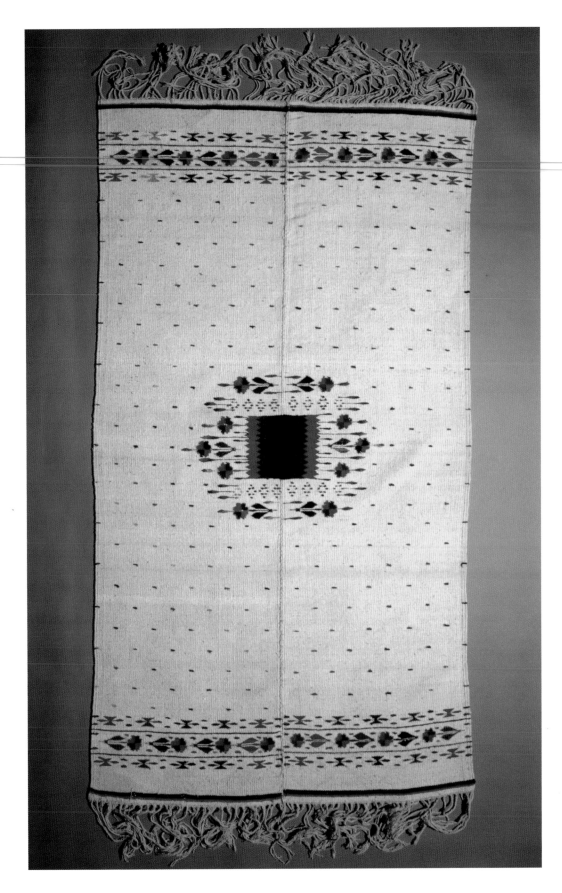

Plate 42
Sarape.
San Bernardino Contla, Tlaxcala.
1930s.
Wool, cotton and linen,
75½ X 38½". MM.

This elegant sarape has a natural background with the design accented in deep red and black. The warp is linen and the weft is handspun wool. This sarape was part of a group of Tlaxcala sarapes that Rockefeller treasured and hung in his summer home.

Tlaxcalans were engaged in weaving long before the Conquest. They were enemies of the Aztecs and allied themselves with Cortez in toppling Montezuma's empire, for which the Spaniards gave them special privileges and favored status. Soon after the Conquest the Spaniards further developed Tlaxcalan weaving to supply their colonists with fabric. By the mid-sixteenth century they were weaving wool, and with the introduction of the treadle loom, Tlaxcala became the first major center of wool production in New Spain. A group of Tlaxcalans was then sent north to the Saltillo area as colonists, giving birth to the Saltillo sarape, whose influence is felt all over Mexico. It is not clear whether the sarape depicted is influenced by Saltillo designs or whether the pattern is a traditional Tlaxcala design that might have pre-Hispanic origins. This traditional piece has a central motif that incorporates zigzags, diamonds and stylized floral shapes. The border design repeats the central elements and contains a popular hourglass pattern.

Plate 43
Beaded Blouse.
The Sierra of Puebla.
1930s.
Cotton and black and gold glass
beads, 18½ X 24½". SAMA.

Beaded blouses from the highlands
of Puebla are used by Nahua and
Otomí women for ceremonial occasions. This striking beaded blouse
with finely smocked sleeves is designed in the same way as a traditional embroidered blouse. From a
distance, the beading is easily mis-
taken for a floral and cross-stitched
design. In times past, Indian
women would bring a few of their
beaded blouses to Oaxaca to sell at
the Lunes del Cerro fiesta. As the
cost of beads increased, fewer and
fewer blouses were seen. Now they
are a disappearing folk art.

Chaquira (small beads) have a
long and popular history in Mexico.
In the nineteenth century, they were
incorporated into samplers and
made into pictures and decorative
cloths. Today they are used for Indian hair cords and jewelry. The
Huichol Indians use them to decorate bags, ritual bowls, wrist bands
and sashes.

the folk art objects associated with these occasions. In the semiarid parts of central Mexico, religious celebration intensifies during the end of the dry season and is designed to curry the favor of those who control the weather and the future of the crops. Masked dramas are performed, special altars are constructed in homes and churches, processions wind through the narrow streets of villages and small towns and sky rockets are sent aloft proclaiming the devotion of those below and as a signal to the gods that they should pay attention to the beautiful preparations of the faithful.

Religious ceremonial folk art is often made as part of a *promesa* to a saint or to the Virgin, who in turn will bestow his or her blessings and good fortunes—health, prosperity and love—on those seeking them. Young women cut their elegant braids and attach them to the figure of San Antonio de Padua, in appreciation for his assistance in finding a husband or redirecting one who has gone astray. Participants in dance dramas perform for hours in order to satisfy a pledge to their patron saint, whose intervention is essential to the maintenance of balance in the world. Altars are built; statues of saints are carved, or retouched, and carefully placed in small chapels; exotic floral arches are set in place; and special foods are prepared in anticipation of the main day of celebration. Folk art is everywhere.

The ceremonial folk art in the Rockefeller collection consists mostly of paintings, masks, incense burners, musical instruments, objects associated with the Day of the Dead and miscellaneous religious paraphernalia.

Paintings

The religious paintings in the Rockefeller collection are among the most important objects in the ceremonial section. There are more than thirty, each a very special example of Mexican folk perspective and expression. *Retablos* —paintings usually on tin, copper or canvas and located on or behind the altar—are represented in various forms. Ex-votive-type *retablos* are deeply personal accounts of miraculous interventions. Made in great numbers during the nineteenth century by itinerant folk artists, these paintings are part of a tradition that goes back to early colonial times and can be found in

Plate 44
Santa Rita de Casia.
Central Mexico.
Mid-19th century.
Oil on tin; tin frame; 9¾ X 6⅞".
SAMA.

This *retablo* portrays Santa Rita de Casia, who is invoked in Mexico as the patroness of desperate or impossible situations and considered a model for married women. In the fifteenth century, late in her life, the widow Rita entered an Augustinian convent in Casia, Italy. In this very tender and youthful depiction, her childlike face, rosy lips and demure look are disturbed by the stigmata on her forehead. It is thought to have been caused by a thorn from a crucifix during intense contemplation in her life of meditation and penance. In her left hand she holds a crucifix, and with her right hand she presses a skull, a symbol of mortality or penance, close to her body.

many parts of the Catholic world. Once painted and sold, they were placed by the devotee on the altar honoring the saint whose intervention is documented by and memorialized in the painting. In many churches throughout central Mexico, walls are covered with ex-votive *retablos*, providing a fascinating testimony to the power of religious personages.

Other nineteenth-century paintings on tin include representations of saints, typically attired in the dress of their time and order, together with special attributes associated with their lives—professions, stations of birth, martyrdoms and so on. The subject of *El Niño de Atocha* (pl. 65), a popular manifestation of the young Christ, is always associated with specific attributes that set him apart from other images: a brimmed hat with a plume, a pilgrim's staff and a gourd, a basket containing flowers, spears of wheat and roses. The Niño de Atocha is the patron to whom people pray for the freeing of prisoners and for delivering people from all types of serious danger.

La Mano Poderosa (pl. 64) is impressive in terms of both its form and its content. It is a fine example of nineteenth-century folk painting, with characteristic soft-edged figures and flattening of perspective. The hand is that of Saint Francis of Assisi, who, according to legend, experienced the stigmata of Christ during a period of intense prayer. The arm is robed in a garment of the Franciscan order. The blood that cascades from the saint's hand represents the blood of the Eucharist. The lambs who drink it are the faithful. At the end of each finger, from left to right, are images of Saint Anne, the Virgin Mary, the Christ Child, Saint Joseph and Saint Joachim. This theme, associated with veneration of the Holy Family, was popular in nineteenth-century Mexico and remains so today.

One of the most technically impressive tin paintings in the collection shows Saint Francis embracing Christ on the cross (pl. 67). This powerful *retablo is* painted in rich colors with a sharply defined technique. The architecture of the buildings at the base is reminiscent of Italian structures and was most likely copied from European models.

Among the religious paintings not executed on tin, the most important is a series depicting twelve of the fourteen Stations of the Cross, dating from 1850 (pls. 68, 69). Station VI illustrates Veronica holding the cloth used to

Plate 45
Ex-voto.
Central Mexico.
1894.
Oil on tin, 10¼ X 10½". SAMA.

The text on this ex-voto reads, "Mister Jorge Cano, finding himself dangerously sick of some illness, prayed with all the fervor of his heart to the Virgin of San Juan for a cure. This small miracle is offered in the month of October 1894, on the Guisache Ranch, for granting me this favor." This small work on tin is an illustrative account of a miraculous intervention resulting in a cure.

In the nineteenth century at the height of the popularity of ex-votos, great quantities of these paintings were executed by unknown, informally trained, and often itinerant folk artists. They interpreted textual material into a very dramatic rendering of an event. Tin was the chosen material, replacing the canvas and copper used earlier for ex-votos commissioned by the wealthy. Devotees placed their small commissioned works on the altar honoring the saint whose intervention is documented and commemorated in the painting. This custom arrived with the Spanish and was immediately adopted by the Mexicans. In many churches throughout central Mexico, walls are crammed with hundreds of ex-votos offering a comprehensive glimpse not only of personal devotion and the power of religious personages but also of the social history and faith and dreams of the populace.

wipe Christ's brow. The attire of the woman on the right, whose back is to the viewer, is reminiscent of Mexican Indian dress of the nineteenth century. The predominant colors surrounding her are those of the Mexican flag—green, red and white. The other eleven paintings demonstrate similar regional qualities.

Finally, the most extraordinary religious painting in the Rockefeller collection is a scroll painting titled *Death of San José* (pl. 66). Painted during the early part of the nineteenth century, it shows, in a wonderfully "folk" manner, a grieving Mary and angels in the presence of the dying saint.

Masks

The Rockefeller collection contains a small but important group of masks from all over Mexico and made of many different materials. Most were used in a religious context. In a time when most mask collections to a large extent consist of decorative and commercial masks made for tourists, the Rockefeller collection is a refreshing exception. Of the sixty masks in the collection, only two were made for the tourist market.

Plate 46
Portrait.
Central Mexico.
Mid-19th century.
Oil on tin; tin frame; 13¾ X 9¾".
SAMA.

This austere painting of a woman, possibly in mourning, is a classic mid-nineteenth-century portrait painted on the standard 10-by-14-inch tin sheet popular with *retablo* painters. It is encased in a more contemporary cut tin frame. The woman is wearing black, a color that was noted by nineteenth-century visitors to Mexico as being the predominant color of wealthy Spanish or mestiza women or children after the struggle for independence. Her necklace, a braided black cord, is loosely draped with a small knot below the neck. She is holding one end of the necklace between her fingers. The classic hairstyle of the nineteenth century was severe, with a central part dividing coal-black hair drawn tightly back into a large bun. Women often wore hair ornaments of filigreed or repoussé silver.

The most important mask in the collection, and thought by some to be the most important object in the entire collection, is a centurion helmet mask (pl. 56). Masks of this type generally date from the late eighteenth century. Undoubtedly, the carving, gesso and painting are of the type and style associated with colonial Mexico, but the mask may well be from the early nineteenth century. Although rare, similar examples are to be found in collections elsewhere—The Taylor Museum of the Colorado Springs Fine Arts Center and the Museo Nacional de Arte in Mexico City. The provenance of these centurion helmet masks is uncertain; however, they are generally thought to have been made and used in an area around Toluca, State of Mexico. Worn to represent a Roman guard leading Christ to Calvary, this mask, with its movable jaw, oversize teeth and ferocious facial features, is indeed impressive. It was made using the *estofado* technique, in which "the wood is covered with plaster, forming a relief design or sculpture, then painted and adorned with gold leaf."[12]

Another outstanding mask in the collection is a Negrito mask (pl. 59) from the State of Michoacán, probably in or near the village of Nahuatzín. Symbolizing that which is good and admirable in life, this mask was used in a line dance, and masks of this kind were worn by several members of the troop. The attached multicolored satin ribbons and glass beads provide a sense of movement to the dance, which itself is usually performed very slowly. One remarkable feature of the mask is the way its fixed facial expression shifts when the mask is slightly tilted to one side or the other.

Another impressive mask in the collection is a late-nineteenth-century jaguar mask from the State of Guerrero (pl. 60). Jaguar masks, still popular in many parts of southern and central Mexico, are among the few masks still used that are rooted in pre-Columbian ritual. In the State of Guerrero, where they are used with the greatest frequency, they are worn in dance dramas related to the agricultural cycle as well as during ritual battles between neighboring communities and barrios. Some jaguar masks are thought to assume the spirit of the animal they represent and to protect the wearer from witchcraft during dance performances. This mask, rare because of its age and fine condition, may well be the earliest example of a jaguar mask surviving today.

Not only does the collection contain masks that are historically significant, it also contains objects that tell us about the often-complicated process of mask-making. Twenty well-worn earthenware papier-mâché mask molds from the State of Guanajuato constitute a significant part of the collection. Although these molds are an important part of the masking phenomenon, they are rarely found in collections today. The masks produced on them are worn all over Mexico during carnival celebrations, particularly in areas where local mask production has died out. The collection also includes several dozen papier-mâché masks from Celaya, Guanajuato, similar to those made from these molds (pls. 2, 57, 58).

Finally, the collection contains objects associated with masquerade dance dramas. A delightfully carved wooden horse associated with the Dance of Saint James (Santiago) is among the most unusual objects (pl. 78). Strapped to the waist, this sculpture is quite different from the more frequently used hoop-style, which slips over the dancer's body and has a horse's rump.

Incense Burners

No religious ceremony in Mexico is complete without the presence of incense, or copal. Dating back to pre-Hispanic times, copal plays a key role in purification and is considered essential for the creation of the proper ambience in which rituals are conducted. The odor of copal permeates churches all over Mexico, saturating the olfactory senses of the faithful while intensifying the visual effect of paintings and statuary. Incense burners of varying sizes, colors and shapes are carried in solemn procession through the streets of small villages, used on the altars of local churches and chapels, and placed on the graves of the deceased during the Day of the Dead. The Rockefeller collection contains several excellent examples of traditional incense burners, some dating from the early 1930s, including a highly glazed, metallic-like incense burner from Barrio de la Luz, Puebla (pl. 51). More gaily painted burners from Oaxaca, Tonalá, and Guanajuato are also represented.

Plate 47
Torito.
Oaxaca, Oaxaca.
Late 1960s.
Papier-mâché, paint, split cane,
and bamboo, 27 X 28". MM.

A Mexican fiesta is never complete
without spectacular fireworks. The
fireworks attached to the bamboo
structure on this *torito* (little bull)
are set ablaze by a *cohetero* (py-
rotechnician), who holds the
sparkling piece above his head and
charges bull-like through a scream-
ing crowd. While the fireworks ex-
plode in bursts of rainbow-colored
sparks, he cavorts with the
high-spirited onlookers. He might
be followed by other *toritos* who
help keep the crowd amused and
moving in an evening entertainment
that never fails to excite both children and adults.

Toritos can be small, or they can
be as tall as a man. The taller and
more complex the bamboo towers
to which fireworks are attached, the
more dazzling the display. Mexican
castillos (fireworks castle towers)
can be many stories high and are often the spectacular half-hour cul-
mination of a fiesta. It might take
more than a week to construct and
fit a large tower with fireworks. This
very technical and precise craft is often passed down in families through
the generations.

Pyrotechnics have a long history
in Mexico, and old engravings show
that *castillos* were being constructed
in the eighteenth century. The
Spaniards brought gunpowder to
Mexico, and it was quickly adopted
by the Mexicans, who were en-
chanted by the magical possibilities
of light and sound.

This small *torito* was purchased
on a Oaxaca street where it was
hanging to indicate the home of a
fireworks artisan. It can be used
over and over again, with only mi-
nor repair necessary between fiestas.

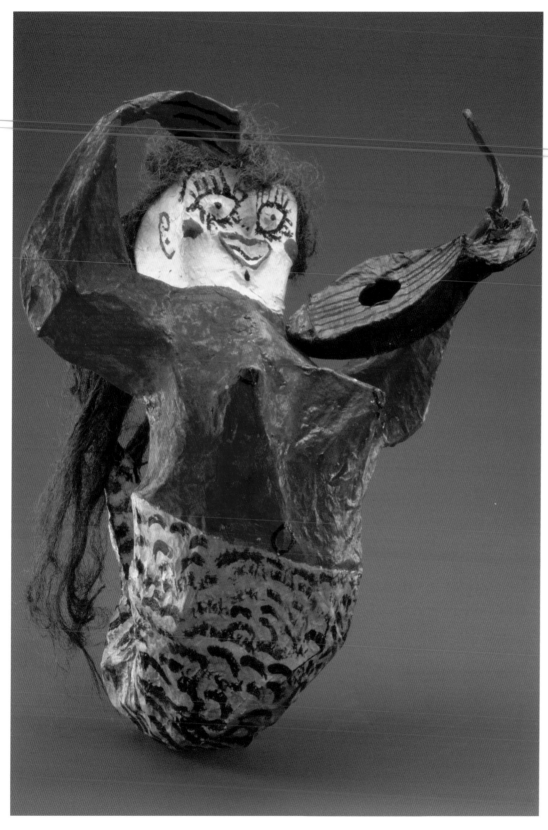

Plate 48
Judas Figure.
Mexico, D.F.
1970s.
Painted papier-mâché and
horsehair, 3 X 2'. SAMA.

This oversize, exuberant siren is a Judas figure, one of the cast of unsavory, nefarious characters that are fashioned out of papier-mâché for Holy Week. The tradition of making and then destroying Judas figures is a fascinating Mexican interpretation of a Spanish custom.

In the old days, on the day before Easter a huge paper Judas figure (often twelve feet high) would be hung up in a village or barrio and then destroyed by fireworks or by burning. Noisy and excited crowds gathered to see the Judas extinguished—a symbolic destruction of evil. This ephemeral art form is meant to be sacrificed. The tradition of making Judas figures is still alive, on a reduced scale. Peddlers still sell brightly painted paper figures of devils, bandits, sirens, evil politicians, villains and skeletons, but today communities rarely get together to burn the oversize Judas figures.

This hot-pink, silver-scaled siren represents a temptress of the most dangerous sort, who will snag the unsuspecting with a tune from her *conchero* guitar and a sly look from her wide-eyed painted face.

Plate 49
Tree of Death.
Metepec, State of Mexico.
1978.
Single-fired earthenware,
42 X 29 X 8". SAMA.

The Day of the Dead inspires artisans all over Mexico. October is a
free-for-all of ceramic production
in Metepec, culminating on All
Saints' Day, November 1, and All
Souls' Day, November 2. This pottery village on the outskirts of
Toluca produces brightly polychromed pottery and elaborate trees
of life. Each year the trees become
larger and more intricate. Metepec
potters have adapted their kilns to
accommodate these trees that defy
tight stacking.

This imaginative unpainted
earthenware tree of death is
crowned with five skeletons, and
atop the upper branches five more
leering calaveras have candle-holders
emerging from their skulls. Nestled
in the tangle of leaves and flowers
are more skeletons—a man and
woman going to market, two men
enjoying food and drink and a jolly
pair perched high up on the tree.

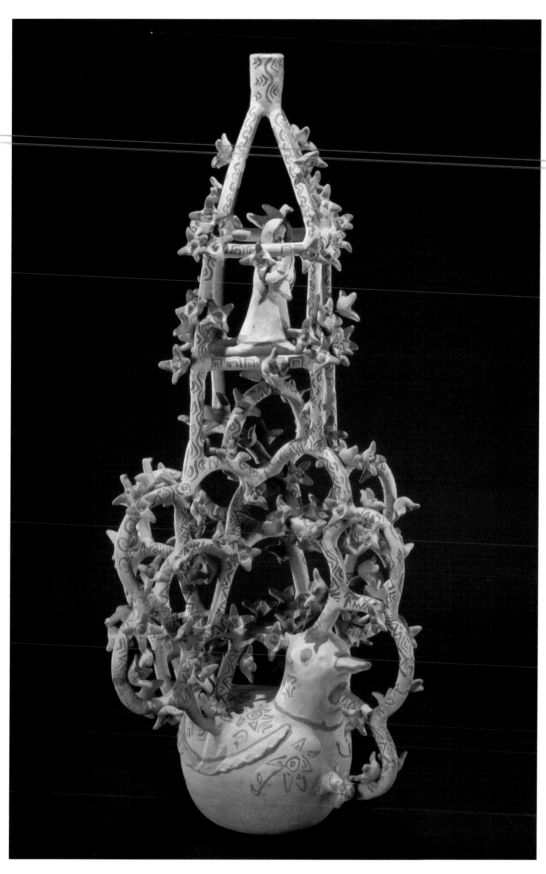

Plate 50
Herón Martínez.
Tree of Life.
Acatlán de Osorio, Puebla.
Late 1960s.
Single-fired, slip-decorated
earthenware, 40 X 23 X 19". MM.

Herón Martínez is one of Mexico's great contemporary folk artists. In this piece he pushed the limits of the tree-of-life form by making it a tree in the round. His home, Acatlán, Puebla, has always been an important pottery center producing everyday utilitarian pottery and a famous barrel-shaped pot invented by Martínez when he first began working. After abandoning pottery for many years, a Oaxaca craft dealer encouraged Martínez to develop new forms. His pieces have influenced the direction of traditional Acatlán potters, who now produce ornamental pottery for an external market. Martínez' work has evolved from single-fired, slip-decorated earthenware pieces to intricate multicolored trees with white backgrounds to his more recent highly burnished slip-decorated trees, insects, wall planters and stacked animals.

This tree employs various ceramic techniques: coiling, press-molding, hand modeling, convex molding and lump molding. The slip, called *tinta*, is obtained from mineral-rich rocks from a mine nearby. Short lengths of galvanized wire hold the tree sections together and connect the leaves and birds to the branches. A complicated tree of life takes at least a week to construct.

Plate 51
Incense Burner.
Barrio de la Luz, Puebla.
1930s.
Glazed earthenware,
19¼ X 12¼". SAMA.

Few religious ceremonies are complete without an incense burner. Folk artists produce an endless variety of containers to burn copal. Copal permeates churches all over Mexico, saturating the olfactory senses of the faithful and intensifying the visual stimulus of the paintings and statuary. Incense burners are carried in processions, adorn home and church altars and are placed near gravestones during the Day of the Dead.

This mold-made piece with appliquéd hand-formed decoration is topped with a crucifix. It was made in Barrio de la Luz, an old section of the city of Puebla, where the Spaniards established potteries under Spanish colonial grant. These guildsystem shops were governed by intricate and rigorously enforced codes. The metallic black glaze is a hallmark of Barrio de la Luz pottery. The form is reminiscent of hanging brass church pieces from Spain and the Middle East.

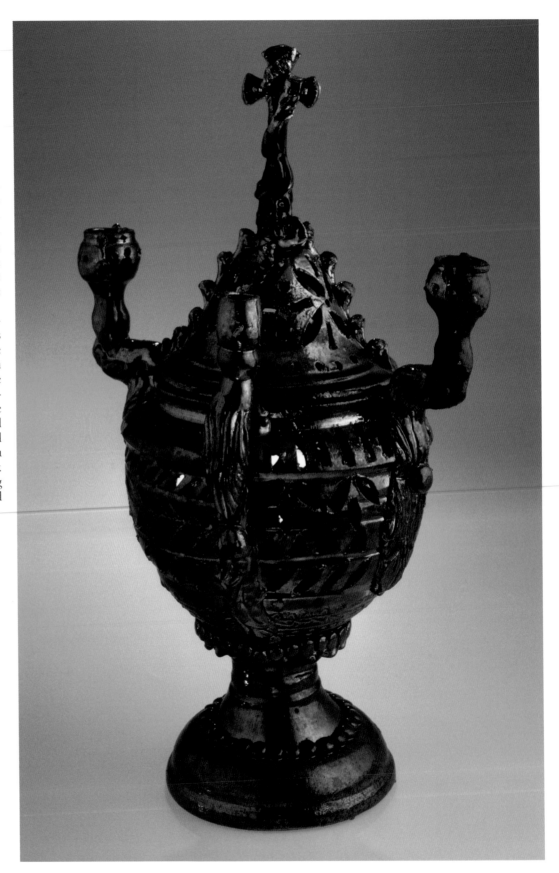

Musical Instruments

Music is another key element in Mexican celebrations. Village bands, comprising peasants with little or no formal training in music, are part of every festival. Participation is frequently due to a *promesa* between the musician and local saints. Flutes, guitars, violins and drums are standard instruments for almost all religious events, but brass and other instruments are also used on occasion. These rustic bands set the cadence for dance dramas and religious processions, and the musicians work hard to make certain that their music can be heard above the din of other sounds in the celebration.

The collection's most important ceremonial musical instrument is a *conchero* guitar (pl. 62) made of armadillo shell, wood, mother-of-pearl and various other materials. *Concheros* are brotherhoods formed to dance in honor of saints or other religious images for the well-being of a neighborhood, community or region. Although these brotherhoods grew up as part of an Indian revitalization movement that began at the end of the nineteenth century, their roots go back much earlier. Each *concha* has its own name and must have been ritually consecrated during a *velación* before its effectiveness can be assured.[13]

Another instrument used in religious celebrations is the *matraca*. Of the several fine examples in the collection, the rarest and most interesting is a miniature silver *matraca* with a dancing figure on top (pl. 52). During the nineteenth century wealthy Mexicans used noisemakers of this kind to celebrate Holy Week. Today, *matracas* made of wood, tin and other inexpensive materials are used by all classes throughout Mexico.

Day of the Dead Objects

Nelson Rockefeller's last trip to Mexico took place during the time when preparations were being made for the Day of the Dead festival, and he purchased many objects associated with the celebration. Although some were of such an ephemeral nature that they have since disintegrated, other objects fortunately remain—sugar animals, candles, bread dolls and tissue-paper

Plate 52
Noisemaker.
Mexico, D.F., or Puebla, Puebla.
19th century.
Sterling silver, 4⅜ X ⅞ X 2¼".
SAMA.

Delicate silver *matracas* were used during Holy Week in colonial Mexico. On Good Friday, the Catholic Church prohibits the ringing of table bells, and during the week-long celebration church bells are silenced until Easter Sunday. Masses are announced by an orchestration of noisemakers. The wealthy Mexicans bought small silver noisemakers for Easter gifts.

Rockefeller bought this piece from a folk art shop in Mexico City owned by Fred Davis. Davis had an enormous collection of these finely crafted silver noisemakers. On this *matraca* a small child is carefully running down the piece, making you feel he will maintain his precarious perch even when he is swung around.

figures bought from street vendors in Oaxaca and the State of Mexico. Papier-mâché masks from Celaya and large expressive figures made by the Linares family in Mexico City are also part of the Day of the Dead materials in the collection. A skeletal figure (pl. 77) made by Miguel Linares in the mid-1970s satirizes a traditional Mexican street peddler who sold small birds from the lake areas that originally surrounded Mexico City.[14]

Another outstanding Day of the Dead object is a large, unpainted earthenware tree of life (including death) from the famous pottery-producing town of Metepec, State of Mexico (pl. 49).

Other Objects of Celebration

Also quite rare and significant are the three wooden molds used for making tortillas (pl. 53). The special tortillas made on this type of mold made only in Vizarrón, Querétaro—are served at family reunions and religious events.[15] These examples were purchased in the late 1960s for inclusion in the Museum of Primitive Art exhibition.

Other ceremonial objects in the collection include ordinary and fancy candles, altar textiles and Huichol *tablas*.

OBJECTS OF PLAY AND FANTASY

A third, large and important category in the Rockefeller collection is made up of objects whose primary function is to entertain and amuse. Consisting mainly of toys—some of which originated in pre-Columbian and colonial times—this folk art is made and used all over Mexico, in cities and villages, by old and young alike. Here, Mexican artists are at their best, being free to respond to the world around them both in traditional and in often delightfully spontaneous ways. A quickly whittled twig becomes a lurching iguana, a deftly pinched lump of clay changes a figure's facial expression and a string transforms a bundle of cloth into a dancing rag doll. Charlene Cerny, director of the Museum of International Folk Art in Santa Fe, New Mexico, observes:

Plate 53
Tortilla Molds.
Vizarrón, Querétaro.
1930s.
Carved wood, approximately
10 X 2". MM and SAMA.

Tortillas, the staff of Mexican life, are consumed in all states of the country. The clapping of hands making tortillas is one of the rhythms of everyday life in Mexico, or at least it was. In many towns and villages the thin round pancake made of *masa harina* (corn flour) is now processed from start to finish by a machine at the *tortillería*. But in the recent and distant past, tortilla making was an important part of a woman's daily life. These tortilla molds, unique to Vizarrón, are made of hand-carved mesquite with animal, religious, patriotic and floral motifs. Carefully and colorfully decorated tortillas made in these molds were used for religious ceremonies and family celebrations.

Plate 54
Milagros.
Late 19th, early 20th century.
Milagros: silver, ½" to 1" X $\frac{1}{32}$" X
$\frac{1}{16}$"; case: tin, glass and velvet,
26 X 16 X 3". SAMA.

This tin mirrored frame topped by
an angel houses a collection of nine-
teenth- and early-twentieth-
century silver *milagros*. In gratitude
for a cure, a recovery or a miraculous change in a difficult situation,
a devout Mexican will buy a *milagro*
from one of the many vendors seen
outside of churches and hang it inside the church as an offering to the
appropriate saint.

Arms, legs, hands, eyes,
huaraches, women's heads, burros,
pigs and praying figures are popular
subjects for a silversmith. The small
silver pig might have been offered
by an individual to thank a saint
for a pig's recovery from infection.
Or perhaps the pig had many
piglets, and the owner felt divine intervention accounted for its fertility.
Kneeling figures indicate that a
prayer was successfully answered.

From the sixteenth to the early
twentieth century, *milagros* were
handmade by silversmiths and commissioned by the thankful. Eventually they were cast in silver but
hand-finished. There was an enormous variety of shapes since you
could commission almost anything—a vase, an instrument or
even an insect if you had recovered
from a serious sting. Today they are
usually cast in metal, sewn to colorful ribbons and pinned on
brightly hued cloth along with hundreds of others.

Plate 55
David Villafáñez.
The Glorious Ascension of Christ.
Oaxaca, Oaxaca.
Late 1960s.
Carved and painted wood,
33½ X 25 x 7". SAMA.

This triptych represents the Ascension of Christ, his ascension to heaven at the end of his earthly ministry when he finally entered into divine glory. He is surrounded by angels. Ascension Day is the most important part of Semana Santa (Holy Week), and this piece was carved by Villafáñez to commemorate the great Christian event. He carves many religious tableaux and altars in a highly stylized and deliberate manner. His colors are very simple and complement the purity with which he treats his subjects. He has influenced many contemporary carvers in the Valley of Oaxaca.

Plate 56
Centurion Helmet Mask.
State of Mexico.
Late 18th century.
Wood, gesso, paint and gold leaf,
15½ X 10 X 13". SAMA.

This eighteenth-century centurion helmet mask is one of the oldest and rarest pieces in Rockefeller's collection. It represents a member of the Roman guard that led Christ to Calvary. It is one of the few remaining masks of this type in existence. These masks are attributed to the Valley of Toluca in the State of Mexico.

This powerful piece is carved of wood and covered with thick gesso. The gesso can also be carved before the piece is painted and gold-leafed. The jaw is articulated with leather straps allowing the dancer to move the mouth and appear more menacing.

Plates 57 and 58
Mask Molds and Masks.
Celaya, Guanajuato.
1930s to 1960s.
Molds: earthenware; masks:
painted papier-mâché;
10½ X 6". MM and SAMA.

Ceramic molds are used to make the famed papier-mâché masks sold in Mexican markets for fiestas and holidays. They reflect the Mexicans' obsession with celebration and transformation and connect both children and adults with ritual. Skeletons are made for the Day of the Dead, Moors and Spaniards for Carnival, *viejitos* (old men) for the Dance of the Old Men and devils and an entire imaginative zoo of animals for other celebrations.

These classic molds, saturated with animal fat, have an extraordinary patina built up over years of use. The masks are made by pressing two or three layers of papier-mâché onto the mold; when dry, the mask is lifted off the mold. Masks are first painted with calcium carbonate, and then the real decoration begins as mask makers' fantasies are unleashed. The accenting red and black paint often appears glossy since the pigments are mixed with *cola*, a gelatinous fish mucilage. It is interesting to note that in the classic period of Teotihuacán, molds were being used to cast clay heads and figures. Well over fifteen hundred years ago, the Mexicans found an expedient way to fulfill a popular demand.

Plate 59
Negrito Mask.
Area of Nahuatzín, Michoacán.
1930s.
Carved and lacquered wood, silk
ribbons, cloth, beads and foil, 4'
(with ribbons). SAMA.

This splendid mask, with four feet
of cascading silk ribbons, a profusion of cloth flowers, and beaded
and foil adornments, is worn for
the Danza de los Negritos (Dance of
the Black Men) in Michoacán. The
lacquered mask has European features and is associated with wealth
and power.

Black people have a long and extensive history in Mexico, particularly in Michoacán. They were
brought there as slaves by the Spanish colonists and imparted great status to their owners. Their elaborate
costumes are recorded in mid-
sixteenth-century writings. When
blacks first arrived in Mexico, they
were perceived by the Indians as
being very powerful and were ac-
corded great status. Tarascans applied soot to their faces before de-
fending themselves in battle to
acquire some of this power.

The first Negrito dance grew out
of religious brotherhoods of blacks
dedicated to the Virgin. The Danza
de los Negritos takes many forms,
with Negritos often masquerading
as clowns, controlling crowds or
paying homage to saints. The
dancers perform many times during
the year, singing or reciting verses at
churches and homes, in honor of
saints, the Holy Child, the Virgin
and village elders.

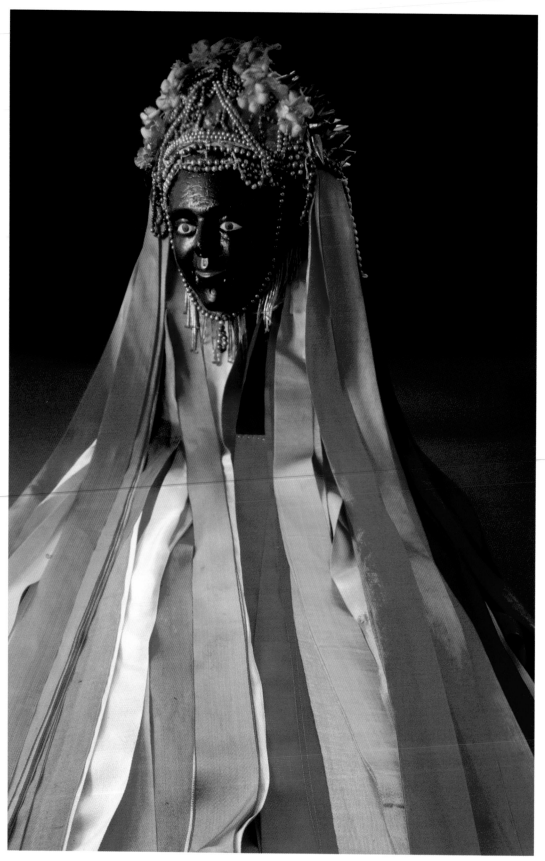

Plate 60
Jaguar Mask.
State of Guerrero.
Late 19th century.
Painted wood, animal teeth,
boar bristle and glass,
14 X 12 X 7½".
SAMA.

Jaguar masks are used in many parts of Mexico. The jaguar was one of the most powerful pre-Hispanic symbols and could be found on Mayan stelae, Aztec altars, Toltec, Mixtec and Olmec carvings, and was depicted repeatedly throughout the early codices. The jaguar, arrogant and powerful, was considered lord of the animals. He represented the night and symbolized war.

Jaguars were connected to caves, to fertility and to the hostile forces of the natural world. The jaguar was considered a supernatural force to be reckoned with. Many versions of the *tigre* (jaguar) dance exist: El Tigre, Tlacololero and Tecuani. In these dances, the jaguar is eventually chased, captured and killed, symbolizing the power to change a threatening world into a pro-

tective one. Often these dance dramas are related to the agricultural cycle or are performed as ritual battles between neighboring communities or barrios. This spectacular mask is one of the oldest of its kind to have survived.

Plate 61
Aurelio Flores.
Tree of Life.
Izúcar de Matamoros, Puebla.
1930s.
Single-fired, painted and
varnished earthenware,
18½ X 16½". MM.

The tree of life symbolizing fertility,
the life cycle and rebirth is a concept artisans find inspiring because
of its design potential. Mexican
trees of life are adorned with flowers, birds, animals and leaves. The
base figure can vary from Madonnas
and saints to Adam and Eve or
skeletons, depending on the purpose of the piece. This traditional
ceremonial tree is made by Aurelio
Flores, whose family members are
the sole producers of this tree and
traditional incense burners. It is not
clear where this form originated, although Flores said they were originally used on wedding altars in Izúcar. He still makes special ritual
trees for yearly ceremonies. Perhaps
the work was inspired by the ornate baroque carving found in the
churches of Tonanzintla, Acatepec,
or Atlixco, Puebla. Parts of the tree
are mold-made with additional
press-molded and hand-formed
pieces. After firing, the piece is
whitewashed with a mixture of zinc
oxide and calcium carbonate. It is
painted with a mixture of aniline
dyes and tempera and then coated
with a homemade varnish of a tree
resin mixed with prickly pear juice.
This gives the paint a brilliant glaze
that eventually turns the base coat
a warm creamy yellow.

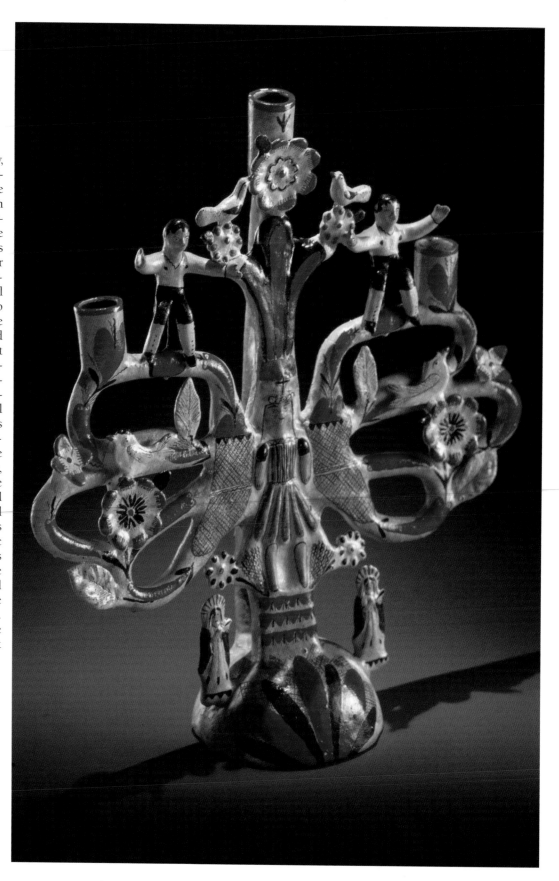

Plate 62
Concha.
State of Guanajuato.
1930s.
Inlaid wood, armadillo shell, mother-of-pearl, wire and embroidered fabric, 35½ X 10". SAMA.

The *conchero* dancers are known by many names: Soldiers of the Conquest, People of the Shells and Chichimecas (after the ancient Mexicans). They are tightly knit and rigidly organized brotherhoods that dance in honor of saints at religious ceremonies and fiestas. *Concheros* adhere to strict and formal fraternal obligations and rituals in their devotion to the cardinal points of the cross. Their dance costumes are elaborate and include ornate feathered headdresses with mirrors, beads, tassels and fringed or feathered layered wraparound skirts. The combinations are a dazzling and showy array of vibrantly dyed feathers, ribbons, cloth and sequins. These dances are romanticized versions of the Aztecs' dances and are closely connected to feelings of nationalism.

During their vigorous dance, they play the *concha*. This twelve-stringed instrument looks like a mandolin but is tuned like a guitar. Each *concha* is consecrated in a special ceremony and has its own name; this one is inscribed with "C.M." A complete armadillo shell makes up the back part of the instrument and is responsible for its unusual sound. Small *concheros* painted on the front surround the winds of the cross. The sound hole is surrounded by delicate inlaid work, and the stem is inlaid with mother-of-pearl. The elaborate instrument strap is intricately embroidered and bordered with mirrors.

En el ex de Mallo de 1851 le aContecio aConceji on Carillo. que hal iendo padecido un fuerte dolor de muelas y en cegida unas juncadas imó allando remedio en la humano, aClamo a S S⁹ Francisco y Jun amente su mina Cruc ta por o que S⁹ a rrestablecida de su salud.

Plate 63
Ex-voto.
North central Mexico.
1851.
Oil on tin, 7 X 10". SAMA.

Ex-votos are small commissioned works painted to commemorate recovery from an illness or escape from serious danger because of the intervention of a holy being. These small paintings are then placed in churches by the recovered or saved in gratitude for the miraculous and divine powers that came to their aid. The paintings by informally trained artists are often incredible renderings that vary from the childlike to sophisticated, from cartoon to realistic, but are always inventive, devout and full of visual emotion. This tradition arrived with the Spanish, was adopted first by the wealthy, and following independence from Spain, achieved widespread popularity among all Mexicans. The ex-voto is often divided into two parts, a charming and pictorial representation of the occurrence and the divine intervenor and an accompanying narrative and devotional text. In this small piece, a woman, Concepción Carillo, is thanking the Franciscan San Francisco de Paula for helping her recover from a painful toothache she was stricken with. She is portrayed in the ex-voto with her daughter. The Franciscan saint is pictured with his staff and cross. Ex-votos are often valuable tools for studying regional customs and costumes. The women in this ex-voto, who look more like sisters than mother and daughter, are wearing traditional *ikat* rebozos from Santa María del Río, San Luis Potosí, enabling us to attribute this painting to north central Mexico.

Plate 64
La Mano Poderosa.
Central Mexico.
Mid-19th century.
Oil on tin; tin frame; 13 X 9⅞",
SAMA.

La Mano Poderosa, an image associated with the veneration of the Holy Family, was one of the most popular and common colonial *retablo* themes. The artist used a painterly technique to emphasize the work's dramatic subject: the hand of Saint Francis, dripping with blood, emerging from a billowing cloud. The blood symbolizes the Eucharist, and the lambs who drink it are the faithful. From left to right, images of Santa Ana, La Virgen María, El Niño Jesús, San José and San Joaquín correspond to the five fingers of San Francisco.

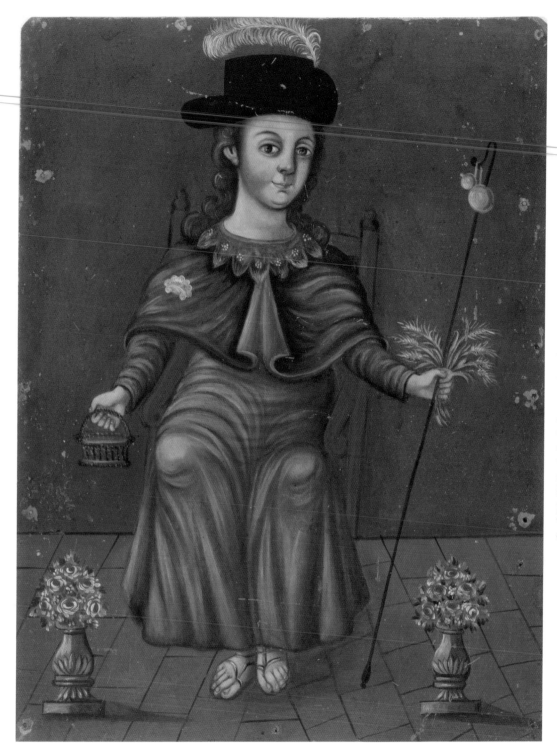

Plate 65
El Niño de Atocha.
Central Mexico.
Mid-19th century.
Oil on tin, l2¾ X 9¾". SAMA.

El Niño de Atocha, one of the most common folk *retablo* themes, is a popular manifestation of the young Christ. This image had its origin in Atocha, Spain, during the Moorish invasion. The tyrannical Moors, so the story is told, forbade anyone except for young children to visit the incarcerated Christians on errands of mercy. The prisoners were starving, and the Atochans prayed fervently for their deliverance. When a young child dressed as a pilgrim with a staff, a water gourd and a basket of food arrived, their prayers were answered. Miraculously, there was still food in his basket and water in his gourd even after all the prisoners were fed.

El Niño de Atocha is the patron to whom people pray for the freeing of prisoners, for protection from violence and for deliverance and rescue from serious dangers encountered during travel. The Niño's attributes remain constant in *retablos:* a brimmed hat with a plume, a pilgrim's staff, a gourd, shafts of wheat and a basket containing flowers or bread.

Plate 66
The Death of San José.
Central Mexico.
Early 19th century.
Oil on canvas; wooden sheath;
32 X 35½". SAMA.

This timeworn canvas, designed to be rolled up into a cylindrical wooden sheath, illustrates the death of San José. Scroll paintings were a convenient way for itinerant priests and friars to carry religious material to the many village churches in their parishes. They originated in Europe to facilitate storage. This painting can be attributed to the early nineteenth century by its depiction of neoclassical bed legs and the tiled floors. The predominant red, white and green coloration reflects the artist's patriotism.

San José's main attribute is a flowering staff, which is said to have blossomed while he was courting Mary. He was selected as the successful suitor because of this miraculous occurrence. The staff also symbolizes the coming of Christ. The staff in this painting is held by an angel. The dying saint is attended by his weeping wife, Mary, while two archangels, recognizable by their wings and footwear, sadly look on. San José is the patron of the family and fatherhood. He symbolizes protection for those in search of a home and for a good death. He is always portrayed as a gentle and compassionate saint. This moving and tender scene is reinforced by the youth and innocence of the angels and by the boyish priest who appears to be an acolyte. Waiting in heaven to receive San José is God the Father, identified by the triangular shape behind his head—a symbol of the Holy Trinity.

Plate 67
San Francisco Embracing Christ.
Central Mexico.
Mid-18th century.
Oil on tin, 14 X 16¾". SAMA.

This *retablo* of San Francisco represents the visionary saint's devotion to Christ and symbolizes the ideal penitent. Saint Francis, born in the late twelfth century, was known for his espousal of poverty, chastity and obedience. In this *retablo* he is wearing the habit of the Franciscans, an order he founded. In 1523 Franciscans arrived in Mexico to convert Indians to Christianity. San Francisco, who had a vision of Christ crucified, received the stigmata during a time of intense prayer and contemplation. He is portrayed tenderly supporting the bleeding Christ while two angels look down upon them. The buildings are a blend of Italian and Mexican Franciscan church architecture. He is standing behind a foliated skull—a symbol of mortality and penance—and a plaque that reads "Charitas HV Militas." The awkward perspective is characteristic of the work of *retablo* painters, who often relied on a verbal account of the subject without a visual prototype to work from.

Plate 68
Stations of the Cross (Station II).
Central Mexico.
1850.
Oil on canvas, 19 X 24½". SAMA.

The fourteen Stations of the Cross, of which twelve are in the Rockefeller collection, recount the route of Christ on his way to Calvary. Station II depicts Simon carrying Christ's heavy cross. Simon rushed out of the crowd to help a weary Christ when the cross became too heavy for him to bear. Christ's arm appears merged with Simon's in a touching artistic gesture of thankfulness. Simon is dressed in red, white and green, colors that emphasize the Mexicanization of the religious theme. A centurion is reining in a very stylized horse that has partially entered the painting from the right. The background, with its curious perspective, the street's surface and the figural highlighting reflect the engaging style of the painter whose lack of formal training never detracts from the descriptive and emotional power of this series.

Plate 69
Stations of the Cross (Station VI).
Central Mexico.
1850.
Oil on canvas, 19 x 24½". SAMA.

Station VI portrays the moment when Christ bearing the cross is approached by the pious woman Veronica, who will mop his brow; according to legend, the image of the face of Christ later appeared on the cloth she used. In this painting, the veil of Veronica has three identical images of Christ, representing the Holy Trinity. Rome considered the three faces of Christ motif heretical, but in Mexico it was a popular way of explaining the mysteries of the Trinity. Veronica and Christ are surrounded by young soldiers.

The paintings in the *Stations* series are excellent examples of the blending of popular Mexican painting and Christian symbolism with regional details. In this painting, the Indian woman on the right is wearing a traditional large, capelike rebozo around her shoulders. Her elaborate hairdo has decorative hair cords and gleams with the sheen of vegetable or nut oils, whose use was popular with Indian women. A red, white and green patriotic color motif is used throughout this series.

VI.
ESTACION

Plate 70
Day of the Dead Toys.
Toluca, State of Mexico.
1978.
Alfeñique and pumpkin seed paste,
1½" to 6½". MM and SAMA.

These delightful and fragile pastel figures are traditional objects made only in Toluca during the last days of October. The recipe for *alfeñique* (sugar paste) dates back to colonial times and combines potatoes, sugar, egg whites, lime and food coloring. The dough is pressed into two molds; the two halves are then joined and decorated.

The rather crude embellishments of these figures account for their naive charm. They are made by a few women who use molds passed down for generations. The animals are also made of *alfeñique,* the parrots of pumpkin seed paste.

Plate 71
Day of the Dead Offerings.
Puebla, Puebla.
October 1978.
Pumpkin seed paste and food coloring, 1½" to 6".
MM and SAMA.

These charming pieces made by a Puebla confectioner are elegant, edible offerings. The Day of the Dead calls forth a burst of creative confectionery despite its ephemeral nature. Temporary street stalls sell sweets, flowers and breads, while local candy shops and bakeries offer brightly painted and tinted temptations. The visual effect is dazzling.

Pumpkin seed paste can be hand-formed, extruded or press-molded, before being elaborately decorated. A woman's delicate hand offering four vivid, perfect roses to her beloved deceased makes a poignant statement. The fruit bowl contains *picante* peppers and some of the ninety-eight tropical fruits available in Mexico.

Plate 72
Day of the Dead Offerings.
Oaxaca, Oaxaca.
1978.
Molded sugar, 1" to 2".
MM and SAMA.

Sweet offerings are just a small part of the culinary delights placed on an altar to tempt the returning souls. After feasting on the smells of mole, tastes of tamales and swigs of beer, it might be time to indulge a sweet tooth and have a fish or a small guitar or a coffin filled with sugar water. Along with the customary sugar skulls that each child buys, these little candies are a cherished part of the celebration and can be eaten with pleasure when the dead souls depart. Often these delicately colored confections are decorated with glitter and foil, turning them into objects to treasure but not to taste.

Plate 73
Elena Carillo and Pablo Cosillo
Hernández.
Huichol Tabla.
Mexico, D.F.
1978.
Yarn, beeswax and plywood,
48 X 96". SAMA.

This complex *tabla* is a contemporary *Nearika*, a Huichol term
for ritual art depicting an enormous variety of symbols and representations used to communi-
cate with their gods. This piece
was made in Mexico, D.F., by

Elena Carillo and her husband,
the shaman Pablo Hernández,
while they were working as in-
formants for well-known Mexican anthropologists. It depicts a
funeral scene of a woman being
sent to the gods as two shamans,
sitting on their chairs, pray over
a quiver containing Tateway, the
old grandfather fire god. The
stars represent the souls of various gods and shamans. The
moonlike disk is the symbol that
identifies the *tabla* as a *Nearika*;
it is where a mirror representing
the central deity Tateway would

be placed. The little buildings
are *xiriki* (gods' houses); each
represents a specific deity. The
yarn colors used are sacred colors to the Huichols.

Decorative yarn paintings are
an urban Huichol folk art not
practiced in their home villages
in the remote and rugged sierra
of Nayarit. Making these *tablas* is
an alternative to the demanding
seasonal day labor on the coast
that the Indians do to supplement their income. The *tablas*,
outgrowths of sacred boards, are
storytelling devices that are very

popular with the Huichol "urban professional artisans" who
have temporarily moved to large
cities. They often work commu-
nally to produce these fascinating storyboards that depict a
wealth of personal and religious
mythology.

Plate 74
Ceremonial Candles.
Michoacán or Mexico, D.F.
1978.
Molded and hand-formed wax, height, 14½". MM and SAMA.

It is hard to envision Mexico without the candles that burn continually in churches and small chapels, adorn home altars and are carried in religious processions, lit for the dead, and used for illumination. Who can forget the magic of a candle-lit cemetery during the Day of the Dead, a nighttime funeral procession making its way through a small village, or an Easter Sunday as hundreds of Indians march with candles and offerings?

Elaborate wax candles are one of the fragile ephemeral arts of Mexico—a selfless art where all is subjugated to the ceremonial purpose. In Michoacán the delicate art of molded wax flowers is renowned throughout Mexico. Multitiered floral arrangements of white wax with gold or silver stamens or pistils might surround a three-foot candle already entwined in colored foils. These candles are a tribute to the artisans who are called for ceremonial occasions to patiently create something that will survive only a few bright hours.

Plate 75
Day of the Dead Figures.
Valley of Oaxaca.
1978.
Paper, earthenware, wire, cotton,
bottle tops and wood, 4" to 10¾".
MM and SAMA.

Each year during El Día de los Muertos
dead souls return to earth to celebrate
with friends and family. The festivities
begin October 31, when the *angelitos*
(children who have died) start arriving, in time for All Saints' Day on November 1. November 2, All Souls' Day,
is devoted to departed adults. In preparation, elaborate altars with foods and
offerings are erected, grave sites are decorated with gorgeous wreaths and flowers and, in many villages, marigold
petals are scattered along paths from
the graves to the altars so the dead souls
can find their way.

Two weeks before the holiday, markets are filled with handmade objects
devoted to death. The imagery is wild
and animated, satiric and humorous,
including sugar skulls and skeletons
from all walks of life. These little figures
are made to decorate altars and for children.

Plate 76
Funeral Scene.
Oaxaca, Oaxaca.
1978.
Paper, earthenware, cardboard, cotton,
fabric and paint; figures: height, 4";
dead body: 3½ X 6½". SAMA.

This small funeral is a traditional Day of
the Dead scene from Oaxaca. Ironically,
the mourners look like skeletons while
the dead person looks very much alive.
The old mestizas are wearing traditional
Spanish mantillas and reading newspa-
per bibles. In any rural cemetery in Mexico you could find a similarly arranged
tombstone. The small cups on the side
would be filled with the favorite drinks
of the deceased, and marigolds, wild-
flowers and burning candles would fill
the pots or tin cans at each corner of the
grave.

Plate 77
Miguel Linares.
Skeleton Vendor.
Mexico, D.F.
Mid-1970s.
Paper, wood, wire and paint,
36 X 19 X 14". SAMA.

In bygone days an astonishing array of vendors sold their wares in the streets of Mexico City. A cacophony could be heard from daybreak to sundown. This lady, disguised as a skeleton, with her baby bundled up in a rebozo, represents a *chichtuilotera*, a traditional street peddler who sold small birds from the lake areas that originally surrounded the city. This piece was part of a Day of the Dead exhibit made by Miguel Linares honoring these disappearing regional characters. The series was inspired by a series of Posada metal engravings portraying a cast of *calaveras* (literally "skulls," but the term embraces all skeleton and skull imagery). Posada engraved a satiric broadside of *calaveras* that was dedicated to women and men at work: making tortillas and tamales, selling chickens and performing all the other daily work activities peculiar to turn-of-the-century Mexico.

Plate 78
Santiago.
State of Guanajuato.
1930s.
Carved, gessoed and painted wood,
gold leaf, and sisal, 17 X 14 X 10".
SAMA.

Santiago, or Saint James, one of
Spain's most important saints, always
appears on a rearing white steed. His
spiritual aid to the Spaniards in their
victorious battle against the Moors
in A.D. 834 established him in a symbolic role as patron saint of soldiers
and of Spain. He was introduced to
Mexico at the time of the Conquest.
In Mexico he led a double life, first
aiding the Spaniards in defeating the
Indians and, later, aiding the Mexicans in defeating the Spaniards.

The Santiago dance is popular
throughout Mexico, and a dancer often attaches a carved wooden horse
to the front of his body to enact Santiago fighting the heathens. This variation of the battle between the Moors
and the Christians recounts the victory of Christianity in New Spain.
This carving depicts the soldier Santiago almost as large as his horse,
which is rearing in victory. His metal
sword is missing, and his costume
blends the pilgrim's cape and hat with
the soldier's tunic.

Plate 79
Julio Acero.
Animal Banks.
Santa Cruz de las Huertas, Jalisco.
1930s.
Mold-made, painted and varnished earthenware, maximum height, 10". MM and SAMA.

In a town well known for its production of piggy banks and ceramic toys, Julio Acero emerged as its most famous toy-maker. Acero, himself a son of toy-makers, produced a menagerie of animal banks unrivaled in Mexico. These animals, which were used as savings banks or toys, were part of Acero's large repertoire, which he sold in the nearby markets of Guadalajara and Tlaquepaque. Acero used an unusual decorative spatter technique in which he blew on the paint-filled brush to cover the surface of the piece with a misting of dots. Few of these banks have survived; the need for money meant that his art was often short-lived.

Plate 80
Toy Banks.
Metepec, State of Mexico.
Early 20th century.
Molded, single-fired and painted earthenware, 8¼ x 13".
MM and SAMA.

These wonderful animal banks are antique Metepec pieces made for Day of the Dead altars. Time has faded the once brightly painted faces, and the clay peeks through the whitewash of calcium carbonate. These mold-made animals might have been models for the *alfeñique* artists who covered their sweet fantasies with a profusion of sugar and potato starch daubs, or is it the other way around? After their stay on the altar, these banks are used to save hard-earned centavos. Very few of these banks have survived.

Plate 81
Julio Acero.
Dog Banks.
Santa Cruz de las Huertas, Jalisco.
1930s.
Mold-made, painted and varnished earthenware; left to right: heights, 9", 10", 9". MM and SAMA.

These mold-made canines, whimsically painted and spattered, have animated personalities achieved by Acero's skill at capturing the playful or pugnacious essence of an animal. Using antique molds, he always managed to transform these banks into unique and vibrant pieces. Since the turn of the century, ceramic banks were named according to their cost per dozen in centavos. These banks would be called "trenta y seis" (thirty-six).

Plate 82
Julio Acero.
Lion Banks.
Santa Cruz de las Huertas, Jalisco.
1930s.
Single-fired, painted and varnished
earthenware, 9½ X 9". MM.

These stately, ferocious, but friendly lions, almost Chinese in feeling, are Julio Acero's finest and most stylized animal banks. Using the antique molds that had been passed down in his family, he created brightly painted, varnished banks in highly imaginative color combinations. Sim-

ply by adding pinched strips of clay, he has given the lion an impressive mane and with delicate brushstrokes captured its leonine essence. These banks are painted with anilines and varnished.

Plate 83
Marcelino Vicente.
Devil Whistle.
Ocumicho, Michoacán.
1930s.
Single-fired earthenware, paint
and varnish, 9½ X 6 X 6". SAMA.

This unusually benign representation of a devil, whose nose is longer
than its arms, is cleverly sculpted so
that the devil's tail supports its body
and also serves as the whistle. It is
certainly one of the seminal pieces
in the wildly creative outpouring of
Ocumicho polychromed ceramics.
The small whistles that were once
made in Ocumicho have been aban-
doned in favor of a bizarre world of
hand-built devils, demons, beasts
and religious tableaux often com-
bined with folk interpretations of
creation, birth and death.

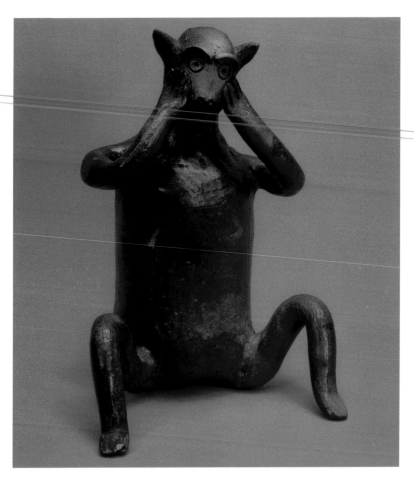

Plate 84
Monkey Whistle.
San Bartolo Coyotepec, Oaxaca.
1930s.
Burnished, single-fired earthenware,
6⅞ X 4¾". SAMA.

Long-legged, leaping monkeys were often represented in pre-Hispanic relief work, paintings and flat stamps and were particularly popular with the ancient Mixtec culture. Monkeys are often associated with the ancient god of pulque and inebriation. The shape of this whistle derives from the traditional Coyotepec black clay monkey bottles that are used to hold mescal. Coyotepec artisans produced enchanting whistles in the earlier part of the century. This small monkey whistle is a sculptural gem reminiscent of the highly stylized pre-Hispanic "caricature" ceramics from Ixtlan, Nayarit.

Plate 85
Corn Husk Dolls.
Santa Ana Acatlán, Jalisco.
1930s.
Corn husk, sisal, bamboo, wood and grasses, approximately
8½ X 3½". MM and SAMA.

Corn, the staple of Mexican life, is grown all over the country. Indians in the most remote villages prize their *milpa* (corn patch), even if it is miles from home on a precipitous mountainside. No wonder the supply of corn husks is so plentiful and put to so many decorative uses. To make these dolls, artisans wrap the husks around bunched grasses, a corncob or bamboo. After being assembled, the pieces are brightly painted with aniline dyes. A tumpline runs around the forehead of the campesino and is attached to *huacales* (cargo carriers) made of bamboo or reeds.

Plate 86
Teodora Blanco.
Animal Band.
Santa María Atzompa, Oaxaca.
1978.
Single-fired and glazed earthenware,
7½ X 3½". MM and SAMA.

These little musicians are zoomorphic representations of a village band. Music is a key element in Mexican celebrations, and local bands incorporate the gamut of musicians, from horn players and guitarists to cellists, flautists and percussionists. Since

participation is often a religious obligation, the musical output can vary from the melodious to the ragtag, from the practiced to the unschooled. Religious ceremonies, dance dramas and local fiestas all call for musical accompaniment, and watching and listening to a band in action are captivating, regardless of the performance, since musicians are above all serious and intense.

These whimsical musicians are a village band disguised as dogs, elephants, deer and frogs. Their scored, striated bodies can be seeded with chia, and if watered they become a band in bloom.

As a teenager, Teodora Blanco invented this veritable carnival of animals in her creative interpretation of everyday life. They have been adapted by other Atzompans and are now part of the large ceramic repertoire from that village.

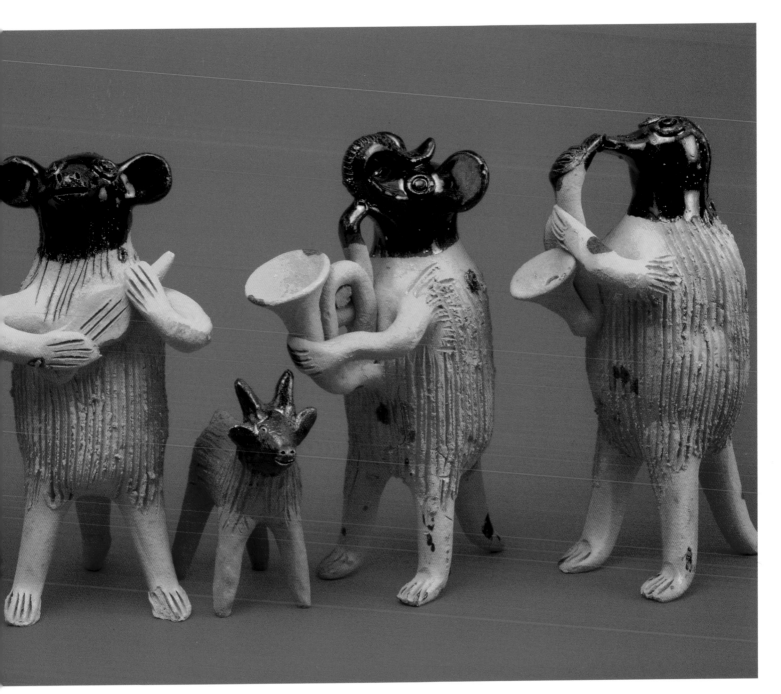

Plate 87
Aurelio Flores.
Vaqueros (Cowboys).
Izúcar de Matamoros, Puebla.
1930s.
Earthenware, gesso, paint and
varnish, 5½ X 3 X 5¾" SAMA.

Antique clay toys made by Aurelio Flores are rarely seen anymore. Although the Flores family continues to make trees of life and incense burners, the small figures of men and women and horses and riders made by Aurelio's father at the turn of the century have almost disappeared. These small figures, partially mold-made, are covered with thick, creamy gesso (a mixture of "Spanish white" and zinc) and painted with aniline dyes thinned with alcohol. They are coated with a natural varnish made with prickly pear juice and a local tree resin. Because the anilines are dissolved, the painted pieces appear stained or saturated. The thick, lustrous varnish imparts a deep and glossy finish.

Horses and riders are common themes with folk artists. These rather amusing variations show a well-heeled and booted *charro* sitting sidesaddle on a *macho* or burro instead of on an elegant horse. The mustached rider is sitting on a saddled, black-spotted red bull, an unlikely occurrence anywhere.

Plate 88
David Villafáñez.
Horse and Rider.
Oaxaca, Oaxaca.
Late 1960s.
Painted and carved wood,
15 X 11½ X 8". SAMA.

David Villafáñez, master wood-carver, is renowned for his unique and stylized sculptural carvings of religious and popular Mexican subjects. His fluid carving and sensual modeling are achieved through an economy and purity of style. Villafáñez' palette is always bright and crisp. His work has had a profound influence on contemporary wood carving in the Oaxaca valley. The horse-and-rider theme is popular among Mexican folk artists; many of the heroes and saints of Mexico, including Zapata and Santiago, are portrayed on horseback.

Plates 89 and 90
Angel Carranza.
Miniatures.
San Pedro Tlaquepaque, Jalisco.
1930s.
Mold-made, painted earthenware and wire, ½" to 1½". SAMA.

Mexico has an obsession with miniaturization. Angel Carranza, born in Tlaquepaque in 1901, was the acknowledged master of miniatures. On his tiny figures, he lavished details that only a magnifying glass reveals. His multiple-figure sets included weddings, baptisms, market scenes and Nativities. These bullfight and *charreada* figures, typical of his miniatures, are perfectly painted with anilines and coated with a mixture of egg yolk and the resin of the mesquite tree to give them a brilliant finish. The figures depicted below come from a variety of Carranza sets. At left, we see a paunchy bullfighter trying to attract a bull with his colorful sarape, a *charro* riding a frisky bull during a *charreada* and a *charro* demonstrating his roping skills.

Plate 91
Miniatures and Toy Whistles.
Various states.
1930s.
Glazed earthenware, painted earthenware, hand-hammered copper and wood, ⅜" to 3".
MM and SAMA.

To enter the universe of Mexican miniatures and toys is to become lost in a world of imagination, humor, color and sound. It is an endless journey of starry-eyed fulfillment and hands-on involvement for children and for adults who are children at heart. There are few countries in the world with such an extensive inventory of simple pleasures. Toys are often vehicles of socialization. In this photograph, the miniatures of utilitarian pottery allow a young girl to play with *cazuelas, cántaros,* bean pots and chocolate beaters long before she is ready to help out at home.

Children often begin to learn ceramic modeling techniques by making miniatures or pieces requiring very small hands. The painted earthenware whistles are turn-of-the-century toys from Ocumicho. The whistle is cleverly disguised in the *cántaro* on the woman's shoulder and the birds perched on their heads. The wooden toys are delicately turned on a lathe and the copper utensils are hand-hammered.

Plate 92
Conchero Pull Toys.
State of Guanajuato.
1930s.
Wood, painted earthenware,
feathers, cloth, cardboard, bottle
caps, paper and fur, maximum
height, 20". SAMA.

The lavish and spectacular costumes of the popular *conchero*
dancers were the inspiration for
these exuberant, articulated toys.
They exemplify a toy-maker's ingenuity in the combination of scrap
materials to produce realistic
concheros, with cardboard *conchas*
with pencil-line strings, bottle-top
instruments and feathered and
furred costumes. Their painted pink
faces with Spanish features reinforce a bearing befitting dancers of
the Conquest. With a pull of a
string, they can stamp their feet just
as the lively brotherhoods of
concheros do at fiestas throughout
Mexico.

Plate 93
Pull Toy.
North central Mexico.
1930s.
Painted wood and string,
9⅜ X 1 X 9½". SAMA.

The spirit of Mexican invention has endless play in the realm of toys. Children and toy-makers are intrigued by movement, and Mexican toys are made to pull, to push, to fly, to flutter, to leap and tumble, to hit, to terrify, to laugh at and to teach and learn from. Toys are made of humble materials with basic tools and with simple and unconcealed mechanisms. Toy-makers know that toys are often ephemeral—that their life expectancy may be a day or a year. But this never diminishes the effort or energy that goes into making these hand-made treasures.

A whole cast of characters is used for push and pull toys, from skeletons and bandits to *charros* and animals. This brightly dressed, pistol-toting *charro*, atop a vivid red horse, is a traditional wooden pull toy made of very light wood and assembled with cord. When the string is pulled, the horse starts riding—fast or slow, depending on how fast or slow the string is pulled.

Plate 94
Push Toy.
North central Mexico.
1930s.
Painted wood, wire and nails,
13½ X 4 X 27". SAMA.

This traditional wooden push toy has a
long handle for a child to hold. As the toy
is pushed along the street or floor, the
wheel, attached to the *charro* by wire,
turns and pulls the rod, giving the *charro*
a thrilling and bumpy ride. The horse is
painted with great gusto.

Plate 95
Aguilar family.
Mothers and Children.
Ocotlán de Morelos, Oaxaca.
1960s.
Painted earthenware, l0" to 12".
SAMA.

These ceramic dolls were probably among the first made by the Aguilar family in its departure from the traditional Ocotlán figures. The women appear to be Trique Indians from the Sierra Madre wearing their heavy woven tube skirts, which have three pleats on either side of the front and are held up by long, embroidered sashes. Many of the first figures made by the Aguilar family in this genre were women with large nursing children. The faces lack the detail of the Aguilars' later pieces. Mouths are rarely more than incised lines or pinched folds, and eyes are painted in simple hollows. These pieces might have been made by the late Jesús Aguilar. They are certainly the prototypes for the creations of his daughters.

Plate 96
Plumed Dancers.
Teotitlán del Valle, Oaxaca.
Late 1960s.
Dyed feathers, carved, painted
wood, fabric and paper, maximum
height, 16". SAMA.

Feather dancers who perform La
Danza de las Plumas recreate the
tragic story of the Conquest. This
historical dance is the Indians' perspective of the Conquest that ends
happily and ironically, when the Indians all become Christianized. The
splendid costumes they wear allow
the Indians to look upon their past
with great pride. Scraps of bright
brocade, shiny rayon, imitation
lace, vibrantly dyed feathers and
small rattles were used by this artisan to portray the elaborately
adorned, plumed dancers famous
throughout the Valley of Oaxaca.

Plate 97
Marionettes.
Puebla, Puebla.
1960s.
Painted, single-fired earthenware, fabric, wood and thread, 7" to 8" X 3". MM and SAMA.

Mexicans' fascination with marionettes goes back to colonial times. After Mexico achieved independence from Spain, European-influenced toys were soon seen all over Mexico. Cloth dolls with porcelain heads and hands were extremely coveted by young girls and were immediately copied and Mexicanized. In many towns, itinerant puppeteers presented puppet theaters for local fairs and fiestas; miniature home puppet theaters became popular. Nineteenth- and early-twentieth-century printers sold broadsides with scripts for home puppet shows, Marionettes were also used for teaching Catholic doctrines in an entertaining format.

In the nineteenth-century, Puebla was known for puppetry and for puppet makers. In a country of toy lovers intrigued with movement, making puppets was a natural outgrowth for the already skilled doll makers. These twentieth-century marionettes are a continuation of a colonial tradition with a new cast of international and national characters. Left to right, they depict a devil, Popeye, Charlie Chaplin, Cantinflas and a soldier. Fine sewing thread is attached to the ceramic hands, cloth pants and hat. The figures can be manipulated into stylized, mimelike postures.

The Mexican craftsman seems to give full play to all creative impulses in the pro-
duction of toys. Perhaps this is because toy-making is not regarded with the same de-
gree of seriousness, as, say, weaving or pottery making, or that a certain whimsy is
not only encouraged but expected. Or perhaps it is because the prototypes of many
toys still made today were inspired by affection for a particular child.[16]

The objects of fantasy and play in the collection are often significant at
levels far beyond that of entertainment and frequently reveal important elements in a society's social and psychological makeup. The widely used
lotería, for example, is pure entertainment on one level, but when analyzed
further, the devils, drunks, scorpions, dandies and hearts found on Mexican
lottery boards can also be seen as the embodiment of the players' hopes,
fears and loves. Popular all over Mexico, buffoon masks are integral parts of
many dance dramas. Often used in scandalous skits, they mock and belittle
that which is sacred and good in a community, thereby reinforcing positive
mores through contrary behavior. Toys of all sorts encourage Mexican children to prepare themselves for adulthood through play. Little girls nurse rag
dolls just as they have seen their mother do with younger siblings. Dramas
of everyday life are played out with toys in a child's private world, not unlike that of the parents.

Mexican toys are also often rich in ethnographic information. Miniature
market scenes, similar to those made by the Aguilar family in Ocotlán, Oaxaca, and ceramic bands from Michoacán and Guerrero are often models of
real-life equivalents, thereby making them invaluable tools for a better understanding of Mexican culture.

The Rockefeller collection of toys is large and varied. Pull toys (also
called trundle toys) from the 1920s and 1930s, earthenware animal bands
from the 1970s, miniature bullfighting scenes, animal banks, puppets and
papier-mâché and rag dolls all are represented by excellent examples.

Of central importance is a set of articulated *conchero* pull toys made in
the 1930s (pl. 92). These lively performers have faces of clay and torsos and
limbs of wood, cardboard, feathers, fur and tinfoil. The instruments they
play are bottle caps. Although the provenance of this group is uncertain,

Plate 98
Manuel Jiménez and unknown
artists.
Toy Musical Instruments.
San Cristobal de las Casas, Chiapas;
Paracho, Michoacán; Arrazola,
Oaxaca; Mexico, D.F.
1930s to 1970s.
Wood, wire, cord and broomstraw,
5" to 16". MM and SAMA.

Stringed instruments of all sorts are strummed, plucked and fiddled by Mexican musicians. Even in remote villages it is possible to find a guitarist or a fiddler. Some of these vibrantly painted toy instruments are for the shelf, and others make tinny and discordant sounds pleasing only the player. The six-stringed guitar and four-stringed banjo were lovingly crafted in the 1930s. The three-stringed instrument was carved by Manuel Jiménez to accompany a musician since disappeared. The red and pink scrap-wood guitars are from Chiapas and are designed with elaborate rosettes around the sound holes. Names or designs take the place of frets or position marks, but the toy-makers are faithful with the bridge and the heels. The simple guitar on the right is from Paracho, Michoacán, where Mexico's finest guitars are crafted. The bodies of the miniature guitars on the lower right are decorated with elaborate broomstraw landscapes and geometric motifs.

similar examples were made and sold in San Juan de los Lagos, Jalisco and Salamanca, Guanajuato, some decades ago.[17]

In the late 1960s Rockefeller obtained a similar set of figures (pl. 96) from the State of Oaxaca—they are plumed dancers, named after one of the many conquest dances for which the region is famous. Other important kinetic toys in the collection include a horse and rider made during the 1930s in North central Mexico, and a larger equestrian set from the same period (pls. 93, 94).

The collection also includes dozens of miniature sets of painted clay and wire figures. Miniatures of this kind are legendary in Mexico and can still be found in astonishing variety all over the country. The best of these were made by Angel Carranza of Tlaquepaque, Jalisco. Perhaps the most splendid example of his work is a tiny bullfight scene—charging *toros*, elegant matadors, daring banderilleros, crusty old picadores—all stationary but with form and color that give them movement and life (pls. 89, 90). Carranza's *charreada* also seems alive with prancing horses, ladies riding sidesaddle and cowboys roping or wrestling ferocious bulls. Miniature scenes of daily life and death from the city of Puebla are also represented, providing humorous and charming tableaux of the city before the turn of the century.

The collection has a large selection of painted earthenware animal banks from Tlaquepaque and Santa Cruz de las Huertas, Jalisco. The elegant lions made by Julio Acero of Santa Cruz de las Huertas (pl. 82) represent the height of his art. Of similar elegance are the barrel-laden mules from Tlaquepaque made by an unknown artist during the 1930s.

Toy whistles and bells from various parts of Mexico are also to be found in the collection. From a historical point of view, the most important whistle is a bulbous figure acquired during the 1930s from the now-famous Tarascan village of Ocumicho, Michoacán. Representing a fantastic devil-animal, this piece (pl. 83) is one of the earliest surviving examples of figural ceramics from Ocumicho. A similarly shaped whistle can be seen in Montenegro's 1948 book on Mexican folk art and is invaluable for comparative purposes.[18]

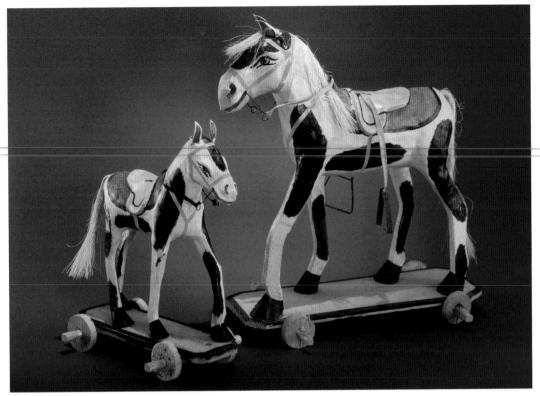

Plate 99
Toy Horses.
Celaya, Guanajuato.
1930s.
Mold-made papier-mâché, wood, leather, metal and sisal; left: 16 X 19 X 7½"; right: 27 X 24 X 12". MM and SAMA.

These delightful horses can be pulled or ridden. They are mold-made and mounted on wooden legs to give them extra strength. The clay or plaster molds are made in at least two pieces. Wet paper saturated with wheat paste is pressed into the molds in multiple layers and left to dry. When almost dry, the pieces are taken out and patched together with more of the paper and wheat-paste mixture. *Cartoneros* (papier-mâché artisans) like to recycle brown paper bags, heavy wrapping paper, old cement bags and newspapers. The stronger the paper, the more durable the piece. The sisal tail, mane and ears are put on before the pieces are joined. The piece acquires its real character when the painter bestows it with individual and spontaneous touches.

The earliest pre-Conquest ceramic toys were animals on wheels. For some reason, wheels were first used for toys, not for their more far-reaching applications.

Whimsical animal bands from Atzompa, Oaxaca, heavily varnished polychromed figures from Izúcar de Matamoros, Puebla, and hundreds of other objects that must go unmentioned, some old, some new, provide additional charm and serve as a reminder of the infinite variety of the folk art of Mexico.

DECORATIVE OBJECTS

The decorative portion of the Rockefeller collection is small and comprises objects that do not fit easily into any of the preceding categories. Created as objects of beauty, their main function is to adorn the home or some other place. In contrast to the objects in other categories, their form is not related to their function, and in this respect they resemble much of fine art except that these objects are grounded in and bound by the traditions of the artisans' culture. Practically all of the decorative objects in the Rockefeller collection, it should be noted, were made to be sold, mainly to customers from outside the community in which they were made.

Plate 100
Ceramic Doll.
Ocotlán de Morelos, Oaxaca.
1960s.
Painted, single-fired earthenware,
3½ X 2". SAMA.

Charming ceramic dolls such as this
one are produced throughout Oaxaca. These hollow, hand-built
Ocotlán dolls bear close resemblance to their relatives on the Isthmus. The pinched and flattened
faces, wide-eyed stares, dignified
postures and floral decorations of
the Ocotlán dolls, the San Blas
Atempa water cooler bases and
Teodora Blanco's dolls exhibit the
transmission and adaptation of regional styles. Many of these figures
are made for the January 6 celebration, El Día de los Reyes
(Epiphany)—the day children receive gifts and toys.

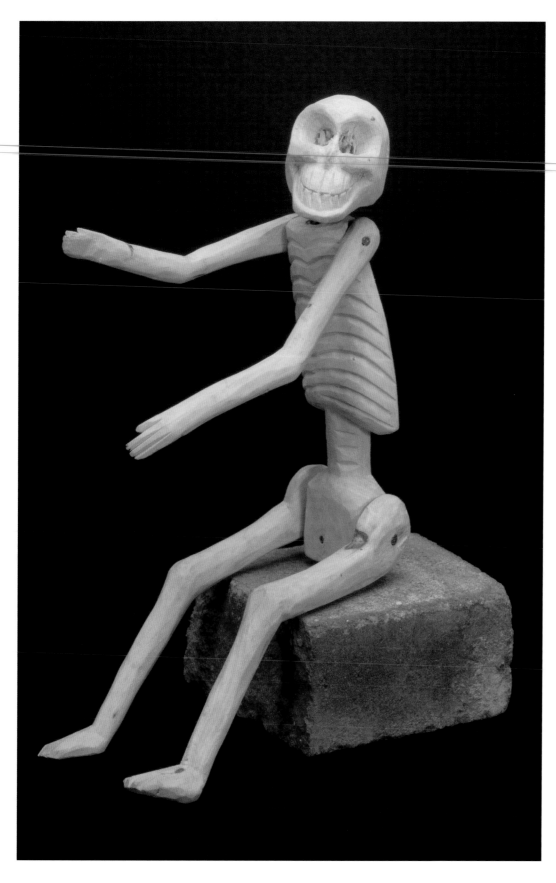

Plate 101
Day of the Dead Skeleton.
San Martín Tilcajete, Oaxaca.
1978.
Carved wood, height, 15". SAMA.

This leering, long-limbed, articulated skeleton is another in the abundant production of Day of the Dead objects. San Martín carvers have recently added skeletons to their repertoire. Left unpainted, the piece's white wood accentuates the skeleton's lack of life and color. This expressive, wide-eyed skeleton can be manipulated into an amusing variety of relaxed, deathlike postures. He looks identical to his pre-Hispanic ancestors, who were often attached to Mixtec tripod bowls.

Plate 102
Wax Dolls.
San Cristóbal de las Casas,
Chiapas.
1930s.
Beeswax, wool, cotton, string,
sisal, and animal hair heights,
4". MM and SAMA.

A set of regional wax dolls from
remote Chiapas represents a curious and by-now-disappeared
folk art. Wax dolls have a long
European history; the most exquisite ones were made in the
nineteenth century. In Mexico,
mid-nineteenth-century delicately modeled wax genre figures, sculpted over a wooden
framework and dressed in regional costumes, were fashionable for the wealthy to collect. In
the nineteenth century, Puebla
crèche figures were fashioned of
solid beeswax. Although bee-
keepers are found even in the remote mountains, beeswax is
now only occasionally used.

Viewing this assemblage of
figures is like visiting the market
in San Cristobal de las Casas,
where a great diversity of regional costumes can be observed
and many local dialects heard.
This area, so rich in contemporary Mayan textiles, is one of the
few places in Mexico where
weaving still plays a central role
in the lives of women. This
group of dolls represents Indians from Chamula, Zinacantan,
Tenejapa and Santa Magdalena,
with their variety of layered garments, sisal bags, headware, jewelry and sashes. The heavy,
handwoven wool is necessary in
the Mayan highlands where
mountain weather is chilling.
The handwoven cotton
quechquémitls and embroidered
blouses are faithful replicas of
women's clothing.

Plate 103
Palm Leaf Figures.
Santa María Chicmecatitlán, Puebla.
1930s.
Woven and dyed palm leaves and bamboo, maximum height, 6".
MM and SAMA.

This group of small people, in town for a patriotic fiesta, is made of woven palm leaves. The colors of the Mexican flag are reflected in their clothing.

The ingenuity of the Mexican artisan is at its height when he or she is working with nature's offerings. Giant palm leaves, bamboo, broomstraw, wheat straw, maguey, grasses, rush and willow branches are all part of the Indians' palette of materials. Palm is particularly versatile; it is durable, waterproof and when green and wet lends itself to almost any kind of manipulation—it can be woven, twisted, braided, folded, joined and dyed. This collection of figures incorporates each of these techniques. Since the palm is worked when damp, it is easy to shape the clothing, the curve of the arms and the stylish rake of the sombreros. Hundreds of thin strands can be made from one enormous palm leaf. *Petates*, rain covers, walls, sombreros, rattles, offerings, miniatures and toys such as these are all created from the magnificent palm.

Plate 104
Plate.
Metepec, State of Mexico.
Late 1930s.
Painted and glazed earthenware,
diameter, 17½". SAMA.

Charros did not court their señoritas atop white elephants in Metepec. The fact that no elephants exist in Mexico outside of zoos did not deter this artisan from painting a very amusing, or perhaps satiric, takeoff on a traditional theme. The elephant is even smaller than the young *charra* to whom the *charro* is tipping his sombrero. Although its pictorial details are unusual, this plate is a traditional form from a renowned pottery village that produces both *loza corriente* (utilitarian pottery) and *barro de cocina* (cooking ware), along with the famed polychromed trees of life, toys and ceremonial figures. Metepec has been producing pottery since the sixteenth century, and the old Metepec market displayed a staggering array of ceramics. The color of fine-particled, rich red clay that is used can be seen through the glaze. The message on this souvenir plate reads "Un Recuerdo de la Villa de Metepec Charritos," meaning, "A Remembrance of Metepec's Little Charros."

Among the most impressive pieces are several large jars and platters from Tonalá, Jalisco. A tall, exquisitely painted and burnished jar (pl. 105) is among the most outstanding examples of Tonalá ceramics from the 1930s to have survived. Its intensively decorated surface reflects the Art Nouveau style favored by potters of Tonalá during the 1920s and 1930s, shortly after the village had become an active exporter of decorative pottery. There are many other fine examples from the same period and place. Stereotypical and romantic images of rural Mexico were often conveyed in this style of pottery; some of the images, however, are less than complimentary. Peasants covered by large sombreros, sitting lazily beneath large cacti, formed a favorite theme.

Another splendid decorative piece is a crane gourd. Too fragile to be a toy, this piece (pl. 125) is among the most beautiful objects in the collection. Edward Weston, who, like Rockefeller, was impressed by these elegantly painted and lacquered gourds from Olinalá, Guerrero, wrote enthusiastically about them in his *Daybooks*:

> *Again to write down admiration for the Indian in his sense of balance, knowledge of anatomy—for in painting and amplifying upon the gourd, actually recreate. The perfect placing of the legs upon the round gourd's body—slightly straighter or more sharply angled, and the fine continuity of line would not have been achieved. As it stands, I cannot imagine a great sculptor anywhere creating more sensitively.[19]*

The large, fantastic earthenware sculptures by Doña Teodora Blanco are also decorative (pls. 108, 115). The basic forms of the figures and others like them were inspired by water-cooler supports from the Isthmus of Tehuantepec but did not retain their utilitarian function. Instead, they became purely decorative objects. Rooted in the legends of Atzompa, Oaxaca, these exotic sculptures depict Zapotec women going to and from market, animals holding other animals and sometimes suckling them, street vendors and a host of other intriguing, often bizarre scenes. Rockefeller purchased dozens of these pieces from Doña Teodora during his last trip to Mexico, and they were among his favorite objects in the collection. They range in size from small pieces of just under six inches to life-size sculptures more than five feet tall.

Plate 105
Burnished Jar.
Tonalá, Jalisco.
1930s.
Single-fired, painted
earthenware,
20 X 17". SAMA.

This large, burnished pot collected in Tonalá in the 1930s is covered with wonderfully stylized and intricately painted flowers and leaves. The sophisticated colors used on this pot are not typical of those used by Tonalá painters today. The raised bands circling the piece pick up the dominant colors for an unusual decorative effect.

The surface of this pot is almost completely covered with decorative brushwork. It is said that many Tonaltecans have a fear of leaving any part of a piece undesigned. Although not traditional, this piece is an example of the exquisite brushwork that had developed in Tonalá by the 1930s.

Tonalá pottery is usually a collaborative family effort, from clay gathering to final burnishing. A piece may be signed by the male head of the family, concealing the participation of women and children. Families in Tonalá have distinct styles, and many collectors covet pieces by the Galván and Jimón families, both of which are represented in the Rockefeller collection. Many of the pieces are made in molds that are passed down through the generations to become hallmarks of a particular family. The burnishing tools used to finish the unglazed pieces are family treasures and are surrounded by some superstition since artisans often feel that the technical skill required to produce a high or low luster not only requires years of practice but also depends on particular burnishing stones.

Plate 106
Lion and Deer Carving.
Temalacacingo, Guerrero.
1976.
Carved wood, 9½ X 10 X 3¾".
SAMA.

An Indian couple walked many hours in the rugged Guerrero mountains to carry these two carvings to the Olinalá market. This sculpture is small in size but monumental in power and concept. Temalacasingo has traditionally supplied Olinalá with a variety of carvings—fruit, deer, lions and toys. In recent years, the artisans have been decorating their pieces with oil-based paints, forgoing the complicated process involved in lacquering. Often the piece's finish detracts from the underlying sculptural forms, which are graceful and carved with an economy of knife, machete and chisel work.

No lions of this sort live in Mexico, but deer inhabit the surrounding mountains. Perhaps this is a reinterpretation of the pre-Hispanic "jaguar eating man" theme, with the head already inside the mouth and the legs extended.

Rockefeller collected three *alebriges* by Pedro Linares in the late 1960s, when the wild and fantastic imagery of Linares' flying creatures (pl. 129) was just being developed. "Alebrige" is a word created by Linares himself to represent these images. They may have been inspired by those depicted in a woodcut by José Guadalupe Posada, but their origin is still not clearly understood.

There are a number of important decorative paintings in the collection. Two still-life paintings (pls. 118, 119) are significant primarily because they are excellent examples of popular still-life representations of the nineteenth century. They are among only a small handful of similar paintings to have survived.

The collection has three canvas oil paintings depicting scenes associated with *charro* activities. Painted during the 1930s, these canvases (pls. 109, 110) reveal the strong influence exercised by Ernesto Icaza, the great *charro* painter of a slightly earlier period.

Among the most delicate and rare decorative paintings in the collection are two small lacquered and painted octagonal dishes from the Lake Pátzcuaro region of Michoacán. Made during the nineteenth century, these

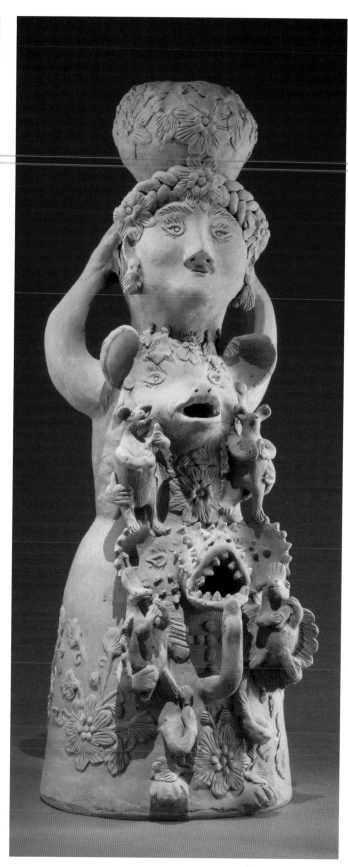

Plate 107
Farmers with Oxen.
Ocumicho, Michoacán.
1978.
Single-fired, painted and
varnished earthenware, 12 X 8".
MM.

Plate 108
Teodora Blanco.
Ceramic Doll.
Santa María Atzompa, Oaxaca.
1978.
Single-fired earthenware,
36 X 14 X 14". SAMA.

Ocumicho's inimitable repertoire of figural ceramics includes bizarre devils, Last Supper watermelon feasts, wild and macabre Day of the Dead sculptures and tableaux of campesino life. Ocumicho work is stylistically faddish and easily influenced by outside demands. These campesinos are planting their cornfield in the primitive and labor-intensive method common to peasant societies. While the father guides the wooden plow, his son seeds the field with oversize kernels of corn. The folk artist who created this piece faithfully portrayed an important event of the agricultural cycle. While Ocumicho pieces are crude and primitive, it is this very naïveté and lack of inhibition that make these painted and varnished pieces coveted by collectors.

This large ceramic doll has curious details rooted in Teodora Blanco's fascination with witchcraft. This piece illustrates her belief in *nahuales*, an ancient concept that each person has a particular animal counterpart that from birth protects and befriends that person. In this piece, the projecting animal heads are the protective *nahuales*, and if they die, the baby animals are there to continue their work. Teodora's art is full of this type of imagery. Her preoccupation with nurturing and the intermingling of animal and human spirits were dominant themes in her later pieces—pieces that displayed a baroque flair for decoration.

dishes are unrivaled in quality and charm (pl. 116). Another unusual decorative object of considerable importance is a half-lacquered and half-painted plaque (pl. 117). This Olinalá painting depicts scenes typical of provincial life in Mexico City. The composition is very reminiscent of domestic scenes painted on Olinalá chests and documented by Jorge Enciso and others.[20]

The collection also contains four exceptionally fine broomstraw mosaics, executed by the late Felipe Olay of Mexico City, who carried the form further than any other artist of his time. The portrait of a Huichol Indian (pl. 120) clearly demonstrates the excellent quality of Olay's work and shows how far the technique could be taken.

Other significant decorative objects in the collection include a dozen nineteenth-century samplers from central Mexico, candelabra and picture frames made of tin, nineteenth-century coconut shells carved by prisoners from Veracruz and other intriguing objects.

The process of putting together this vast and varied collection gave Nelson Rockefeller immense pleasure. It is a vital reminder of his eclectic taste and of his enthusiasm for art independent of its market value. Now, through this collection, the viewer may share in the joy of discovering Mexican folk art at its exuberant best.

Plate 109
Charro Painting.
North central Mexico.
20th century.
Oil on canvas, 34 x 24½". SAMA.

Nineteenth-century provincial life was well documented by anonymous painters. *Ranchero charros*, a new class of wealthy Mexican landholders, emulated the Spanish penchant for fine horses and riding. With money to spend, they indulged themselves in the splendor of exquisitely decorated costumes, bridles and saddles. These mestizo ranchers were the original *charros*.

This very energetic painting depicts the branding and roping skills of Mexico's early *charros*. In the midst of all the activity, a campesino dressed in white is running toward a *charro*, imploring him to leave his cows alone. The two snow-covered peaks in the background are the majestic Popocatépetl and the sleeping beauty Ixtaccíhuatl.

Plate 110
Charro Painting.
North central Mexico.
20th century.
Oil on canvas, 34 X 24½". SAMA.

This painting reveals everything about *charros*' taste in horses and costumes, from heavy felt sombreros to silver inlaid pommels and carved and ornamented saddles. These six *charros* are enjoying a game of cards during a ride in the verdant foothills. No two *charros* wear the same outfit, and the elegant horses are also each outfitted differently. Popular painters were not academy trained but were technically inventive. A clue to the location of this landscape is the strong wind that is portrayed, not unlike the violent winds described by early visitors to the mining districts of north central Mexico.

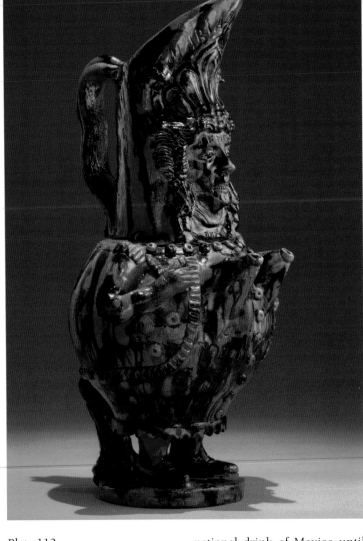

Plate 111
Water Jar.
Patamban, Michoacán.
1960s.
Glazed earthenware,
32½ X 19½".
SAMA.

This heroic pineapple jar is a type of deluxe water container called a *piña*. These jars are mold-made, with daubs of clay applied by hand. These numerous protrusions vary from crude lumps to carefully appliquéd pieces that can be hand-formed but are generally mold-made. In the past fifteen years, the *piñas* have become increasingly complex, with hundreds of modeled leaves covering larger and larger jars. The spiked crown of the pineapple is the lid of the jar.

The origin of the use of these pineapple motifs is not known, although in western Mexico in pre-Conquest time, covered jars with similar decoration were produced.

Piñas can store water or, at times, *tepache,* one of Mexico's regional drinks made from pineapple, pulque, water and cloves.

Plate 112
Pulque Pitcher.
Barrio de la Luz, Puebla.
1930s.
Mold-made, drip-glazed
earthenware, 19 X 10¾". SAMA.

Barrio de la Luz, an area in the city of Puebla where many potteries were established in the eighteenth century, produces highly glazed utilitarian ware. The deep red earthenware is streaked with spatters, splotches and drips of a runny black glaze in a glazing style known as *chorreado*. This large, amusing piece with double spouts is used for serving pulque. Pulque was the national drink of Mexico until the introduction of beer in the late nineteenth century. Written on the front of this pitcher are the words, "María de la Gloria, de Puebla. A todos les boi a serbir a esta umilde reunion. Agosto 22 año 1936 un recuerdo de A. Alonso." María de la Gloria, of Puebla, is the young woman depicted on the pitcher; the rest of the artist's message translates as follows, "I will serve everyone at this humble reunion. August 22, 1936. A memento from A. Alonso."

Plate 113
Bottles.
Mexico, D.F.
1930s.
Hand-blown glass, heights, 13½".
MM and SAMA.

Spaniards brought the craft of glass-blowing to Mexico, where it was quickly adopted. The first glass-blowers settled in Puebla and from there moved on to set up factories in Mexico, D.F., Guadalajara and Texcoco. Pressed glass is made primarily in Puebla.

The variety of glassware in Mexico extends beyond the utilitarian to highly decorative miniatures and toys. The beauty of some Mexican glassware derives from the unusual quality of the glass, often characterized by random patterns of air bubbles that create a sparkle and luster, making each piece unique. Often the coloration is gradated, and the uneven saturation gives the glass a rich, handmade appearance. This commemorative Guadalupe bottle might have been used for celebratory drinks or carried away from a great fiesta in Mexico City as a souvenir.

The Virgin of Guadalupe, Mexico's patroness and most beloved and popular saint, is lovingly crafted and molded in every imaginable material. The legend of the miraculous apparition of the dark-skinned Indian Virgin followed the Spanish denial of cult worship after the Conquest. Her shrine is the holiest in Mexico, and her fiesta on December 12 is one of the Catholics' most holy days.

These bottles were undoubtedly production pieces. Similar bottles were exhibited in the famous 1921 exhibition of folk art in Mexico City and also at the Museum of Modern Art in 1940.

Plate 114
Adam and Eve.
San Pedro Tlaquepaque, Jalisco.
1930s.
Painted and varnished
earthenware, 7 X 4 X 2". SAMA.

The Spaniards brought Catholicism to Mexico along with all the participants of Judeo-Christian mythology. Adam and Eve are popular figures with ceramic artists, who place them at the bases of trees of life and in elaborate Nativity crèches. This depiction of Adam and Eve, missing their apple tree, was made for a crèche. The mold-made figures are identical, except for Adam's beard. Mexican Nativities include a staggering cast of biblical characters in a rural Mexican setting and are not complete without these visitors from the Garden of Eden.

Plate 115
Teodora Blanco.
Ceramic Figures.
Santa María Atzompa, Oaxaca.
1978.
Single-fired earthenware, average
height, 14". MM and SAMA.

Teodora Blanco, one of the most creative and vital folk artists in Mexico, died in 1981, leaving behind a history of unique invention that set her apart from other potters in Santa María Atzompa. Her parents were successful farmers. Although they were also traditional potters, it was not necessary to push Teodora into commercial pottery. As a child she visited archaeological museums in Oaxaca and was inspired by animal and figural ceramics. Her innovations began as a teenager, when she formed animal musicians. She then started attaching wings and tails to pitchers, whose spouts became animal heads. If she was working on a traditional shape, she would always add animal appendages. In her late twenties she began making her legendary figures of women, such as those seen in this photograph. Her figures constantly evolved and changed as she experimented with various combinations of women, animals and mythical creatures. Beasts poked out of abdomens, breasts became animal heads and animals and babies tugged at shoulders and skirts. Teodora's impulse for surface adornment was intense, and by the late 1970s her figures were covered with appliquéd coils, animals emerging from the bodies and arms typically engaged in holding or carrying children, animals or market baskets. In spite of all this sculptural abandon, her women are always dignified and elegant. For Teodora, the only reason to live was to make pottery.

Rockefeller was truly captivated by Teodora's artistic energy, humor and dedication to her personal vision. He started collecting her work in the late 1960s. During his final visit to her house in 1978, he bought every ceramic doll she had.

Plate 116
Lacquered Dish.
Pátzcuaro, Michoacán.
19th century.
Lacquered wood and gold leaf,
diameter, 7½". SAMA.

Michoacán has a great and ancient
tradition of lacquerware dating back
to the sixteenth century. This exquisite piece, acquired in the 1930s,
was made in the middle to late
nineteenth century. The portrait of
the young woman is delicate and
stylized. The rose, held in an almost Hindu pose, seems to sym-
bolize the blush and ripeness of her
youth. The rosy hue of the flower is
reflected on her face. The feathery
brushstrokes in the surrounding
motif complement her femininity.
The colors are all natural pigments
ground by hand on a metate according to guild traditions. Formulas for making pigments and lacquer are often well-guarded family
secrets. This is one of the rarest
pieces in the Rockefeller collection,
as very few of these fragile dishes
have survived.

Plate 117
Lacquered Plaque.
Olinalá, Guerrero.
Early 20th century.
Lacquered and painted wood,
9½ X 6½". SAMA.

This unusual plaque is a curious mix of portraiture and ironic social commentary on nineteenth-century life. The *funcionario* (bureaucrat) with quilled pens and a small ink jar, ready to sign away someone's land, is loyally attended by two barefoot women in European dress and holding parrots. This scene was not indigenous to Olinalá but was probably copied from a book or a postcard. The plaque is executed in the *rayado* (incised) technique. After the first coats of lacquer and pigment have been applied and polished, another coat is applied. While this coat is still damp, the artist incises the design with a thorn. The areas of the undercoat to be exposed are revealed by the delicate removal of the sections of the outer layer within the incised lines. Each time-consuming step is performed by a different specialist. In this piece, the three figures were painted on after the lacquerwork was completed.

Plate 118
Still Life.
State of Puebla.
Mid-19th century.
Oil on canvas, 22 X 30". SAMA.

Nineteenth-century popular painting —portraits, still lifes and landscapes—reveals much about day-to-day life in colonial Mexico.

This charming painting of a fiesta table depicts an assortment of the wondrous sweet breads available from Mexican *panaderías* (bakeries), where breads and rolls of every shape and size are part of daily life. This mound of goodies might include "cat's ears," "butterflies," "partridge eyes," "neckties" or any other of the three hundred varieties of breads available in Mexico. Artfully arranged on a Talavera platter, the breads are adorned with *papel picado* (punched foil and tissue paper) decorative flags that are made in San Salvador Huixcolotla, Puebla. The elegant decanters and heavy, silver filigreed jar holder are clues to the wealth of the owners.

Plate 119
Still Life.
State of Puebla.
Mid-19th century.
Oil on canvas, 22 X 30". SAMA.

This still life depicts a parrot and a Talavera platter overflowing with Mexican fruits—*zapote blanco, piña (pineapple), tuna* (fruit of the prickly pear cactus), mangoes, limes, apples, bananas and grapefruits. Parrots were often pets of upper-class families, and the small pitcher from Barrio de la Luz is a clue to a Puebla locale.

Plate 120
Felipe Olay.
Portrait.
Mexico, D.F.
1930s.
Broomstraw, wax, and aniline dyes; gold-leaf frame; 10 X 8".
SAMA.

Felipe Olay's faithful portrait of a Huichol Indian from the Sierra de Nayarit is a most unusual example of the disappearing art of *popote. Popoteros* were not uncommon in the late 1800s, but today only a few craftsmen are working in Mexico City. Olay was considered Mexico's finest practitioner of this art.

These intricate mosaics of hollow broomstraw require many tiny pieces to be precisely inlaid on a thin layer of wax that overlays a drawing. The artist tints the *popote* with vegetable or aniline dyes mixed with boiling water. Once dry, it is cut into thousands of small pieces according to the design. Seen at a distance, this portrait appears to be a painting. Up close, the intricate mosaic of broomstraw leaves you in awe of the imagination and skill that pieced it together.

The Huichol Indian portrayed in this piece is accurate in every regional nuance. The detail in his hat makes it appear to be handwoven. The sinews of his arms and the lines in his face impart the nobility, fortitude, and strength necessary to survive in the remote mountains.

Plate 121
Jar.
Tonalá, Jalisco.
1930s.
Single-fired, painted and
burnished earthenware, 31 X 21".
SAMA.

Tonaltecan pottery dating back at
least to the seventeenth century is
famous for its exquisite brush painting and for its aromatic clay. *Loza
del Olor* (aromatic ceramic ware) is
famous throughout Mexico for the
flavor it imparts to the water stored
within. In the early twentieth century, some Tonalá pottery was elaborately painted with very fine and
feathery brushstrokes almost Chinese or Persian in the attention to
detail and style. Tonaltecan pottery
is burnished before it is fired. This
piece epitomizes the fabulous artistic experimentation and a subtle departure from traditional color and
design. The allover floral motifs are
painted with natural pigments
mined in the Tonalá vicinity.

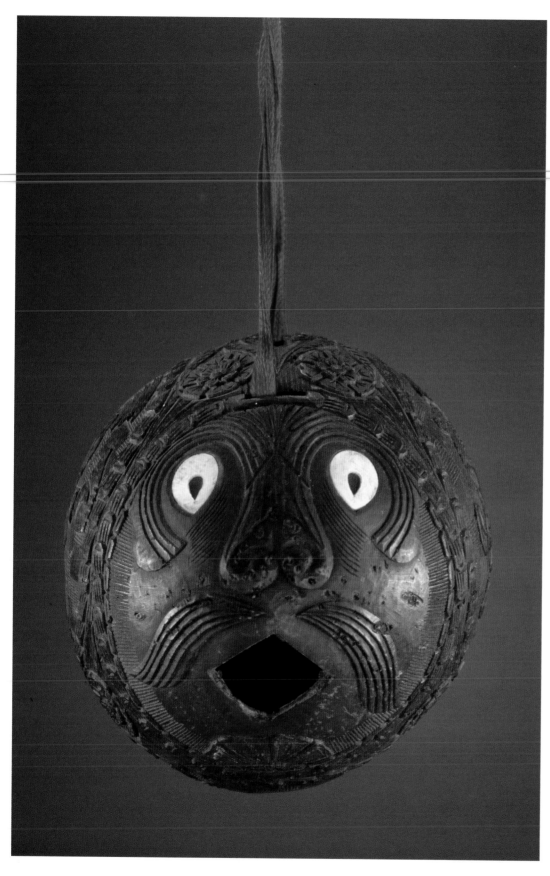

Plate 122
Carved Coconut Bank.
Veracruz, Veracruz.
Late 19th century.
Carved coconut, 6 X 5". SAMA.

Coconuts, mamey pits and walnut shells have all intrigued carvers. This coconut shell representing a mustached feline has inlaid mother-of-pearl eyes. The head is framed with a motif of pre-Hispanic hands, and the remaining coconut is carved with a man holding a mug or bottle on one side and on the other a patriotic eagle and serpent. These pieces were made in the San Juan de Ulúa jail in Veracruz or regional jails in Tabasco. Mexican inmates often spend hours each day engaged in a craft that can be sold by their relatives to supplement the family income or by the prisoner to supplement his fond allowance. It is not unusual for the prisoner to discover a new talent while doing time. Prisoners often used the items they made as ex-votos: the carver would depict his crime on one side of the piece and, on the other side, the saint to whom he was asking forgiveness.

Plate 123
Josefina Aguilar.
Ceramic Figures.
Ocotlán de Morelos, Oaxaca.
1970s.
Hand-formed, single-fired painted
earthenware, average height, 22".
SAMA.

These large ceramic figures by Josefina Aguilar are from the set that
had been displayed on the Aguilar
picket fence and which Rockefeller
bought in its entirety during his
1978 trip to Oaxaca. They are part
of a cast of regional dolls that she
enjoyed making and that lent themselves to various techniques in
hand-forming and modeling. The
woman on the left is probably from
the Mixteca Alta of Oaxaca, evidenced by the wrapping and pleat-
ing of her tube skirt worn with an
embroidered belt. She is wearing a
large necklace and earrings representative of the filigreed gold jewelry popular in Oaxaca and often included in a Zapotec woman's dowry
in Tehuantepec. A rosary is draped
in her hand and a rebozo over her
shoulder. She combines many of
Oaxaca's regional details. The man,
wearing traditional cotton pants
and huaraches, is proudly holding
his *cobija* (blanket). He might be
from San Sebastián Peñoles, Oaxaca, where the blanket borders typically are colored orange, red and
dark brown. Aguilar molded for
him a belt and a scarf that is tied
around his neck. She painted his
face a dark color. Is he from the
coast of Oaxaca or nearby? These
figures were ceramic samplers for
Aguilar's experimentation with the
wealth of regional differences she
observed in her market town. Most
important, she instilled these figures
with great dignity and character.

152▲▲

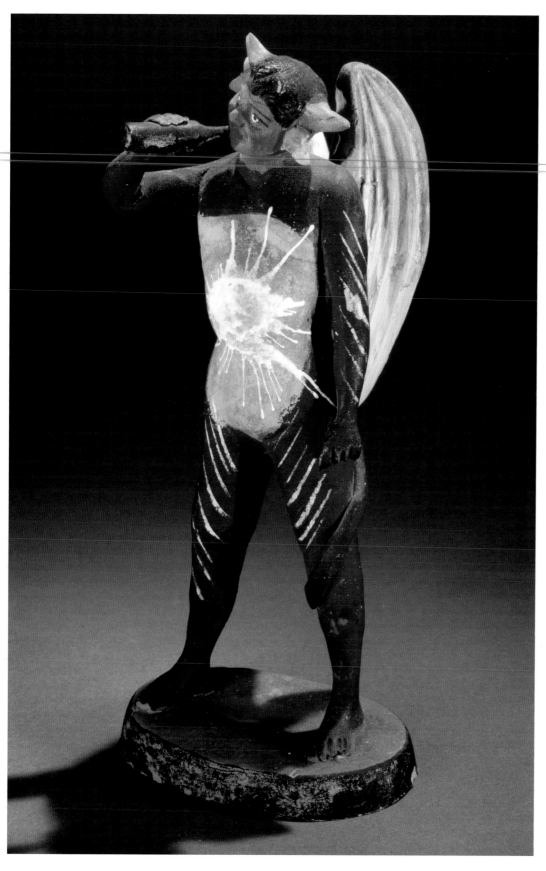

Plate 124
Devil.
San Pedro Tlaquepaque, Jalisco.
1930s.
Painted earthenware, 11 x 3".
SAMA.

Mold-made devils from Tlaquepaque are fashioned for crèches and represent the evils of temptation. They are painted in lurid colors and often have prominent ribs, clenched fists and a tail wrapping around the leg and ending beneath the knee. Set off to one side, lurking in the moss-covered crèche, the devils' outrageous and wonderful color combinations vibrate visually in contrast to the more serious subject of the Nativity. This devil with his spontaneous splotch of paint has the additional vice of drink.

Plate 125
Lacquered Crane.
Olinalá, Guerrero.
Collected in the 1930s.
Lacquered and painted gourd;
wooden legs and base; 22 X 15 X 6".
SAMA.

This perfectly balanced, graceful crane was one of Nelson Rockefeller's favorite pieces. Made of a lacquered gourd, its spindly, reed-thin legs are carved of wood. With all of its fragility this crane has survived a long migration and a variety of owners, beginning in the mid-1920s. The early luminaries of the Mexican popular arts renaissance treasured this piece, which was first shown at the Metropolitan Museum in New York at the 1930 *Mexican Arts* exhibition, designed by René d'Harnoncourt.

Gourds have been used by artisans throughout Mexican history. Their multitude of shapes have produced an equal variety of uses, from the most logical and enduring water vessels and bowls to storage containers, hats, rattles and decorative objects. Lacquering is one of Mexico's oldest arts, and fragments of colored gourds have been found in ancient tombs. Gourds are still used in many parts of Mexico as canteens and, when cut into bowl shapes, to hold hot drinks and gruel.

Preparing a gourd so that it is dry and smooth enough to hold lacquer is a long and time-consuming process. The base coat, usually made with chia seed oil, is covered by powdered dolomite and burnished. Then the ground pigments are applied and burnished to a brilliant sheen. The layer can be thin, or it can be built up to produce a thick coat. Burnishing a gourd is extremely difficult because of its curved surface.

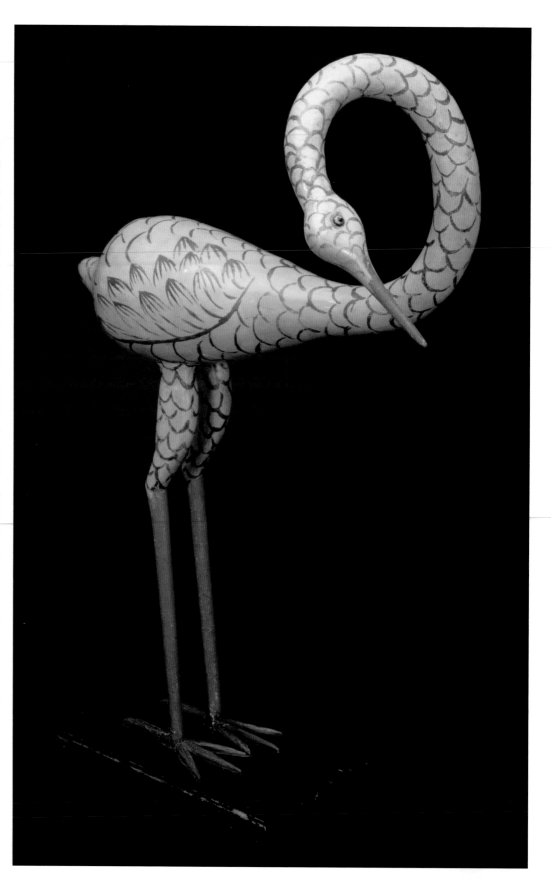

Plate 126
Manuel Jiménez.
Wood Animals.
Arrazola, Oaxaca.
Late 1960.
Painted wood, maximum
height, 8".
Destroyed by insects while in
storage in the early 1980s.

These brightly painted wood animals were made by a former adobe mason and bracero cane cutter, who started carving for his own pleasure. Jiménez recalls that as a small boy he loved tending animals. When he was out in the fields he would often fashion small figures from streambed mud. He sees these small toys he made as a boy as the beginning of his art. When he began carving wood, there was little call for his work, aside from an occasional need for a mask or a *santo* (saint) in his village. He brought his earliest pieces to a vendor in the Oaxaca market and was soon discovered by tourist shops. Jiménez uses a *tsompanclé* wood, from a tree found in the surrounding mountains. He carves the pieces when the wood is green and soft enough to work. He uses a machete for roughing out the animal and a knife for fine carving. Legs, arms and ears are carved separately and nailed on. Jiménez now uses chisels, awls, rasps and drills, but his early pieces were simply carved. His animals are always captivating. Their expressions are imploring, and the curves of their bodies suggest subtle and interesting movement. With an economy of machete strokes he managed to transform a branch into an engaging animal with an abundance of energy. He painted these animals with bright and primary aniline colors. These pieces are typical of his favorite palette in the late 1960s. In addition to animals, he carved large Nativity scenes, sirens, Madonnas and devils. His highly acclaimed carvings are collected internationally.

Plate 127
Panduro family.
Fruit and Market Vendors.
San Pedro Tlaquepaque, Jalisco.
1930s.
Single-fired, mold-made
earthenware, painted and
varnished, 6¾ X 5 X 4". MM
and SAMA.

In elaborate crèches, every aspect
of traditional Mexican life is represented. Mexican families pride

themselves on the size of their
crèches, which frequently have
over one hundred figures. Market
vendors such as these are often
present in Nativity scenes. Tlaquepaque artisans work all year to
make these figures for the Christmas rush, and during November
they bring their wares to markets
throughout Mexico.

The Panduro family molds
have been used for generations.
The finer the original mold, the

more intricate the figures. The
painting of mold-made objects
often determines their quality,
and the Panduros are noted for
their careful brushwork and attention to detail. Aniline dyes
fixed with egg yolk were used as
paint. Today many artisans prefer airbrushing their figures with
commercial oil-based or vinyl
paint. The ceramic fruit banks in
the foreground of this arrange-
ment can be strung up on altars

or used to save centavos. These
vividly painted banks are made
in every variety of delectable
tropical and regional fruit.

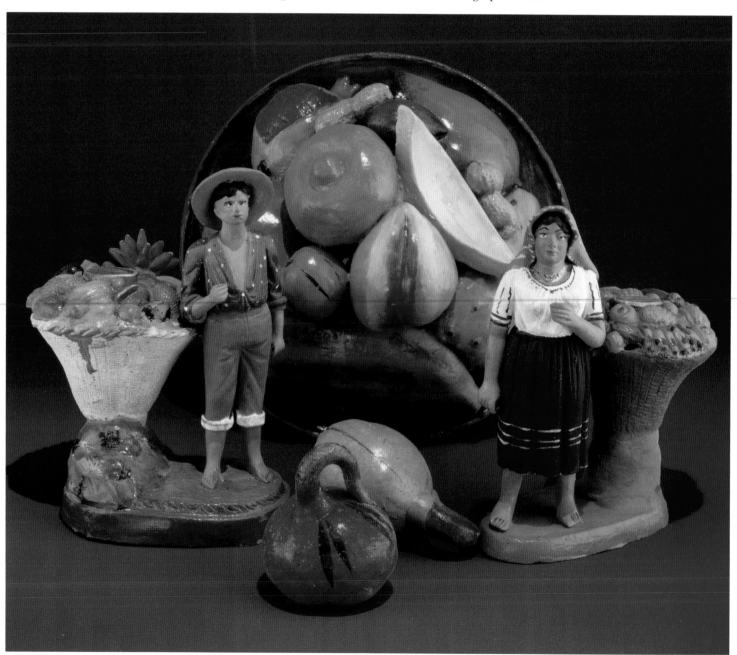

Plate 128
Wooden Containers.
San Antonio de la Isla, State of Mexico.
1930s.
Turned and incised wood, carved bone handles and feet; left to right: 4¼ X 4", 6 X 4", 4¾ X 3½". MM and SAMA.

These delicate polished and chiseled wooden boxes are made in a small village near Toluca. San Antonio de la Isla has many craft traditions: carving cattle-horn combs, turning *molinillos* (chocolate beaters) and making wooden boxes incised with flowers, animals and geometric designs.

In the early part of the century, these boxes were turned on primitive foot-powered lathes and then incised with chisels. The tops were inlaid, and the bone knobs were whimsically carved with birds, animals and faces. Today more sophisticated tools have replaced much of the hand carving, but the small boxes with their tight-fitting lids are still used to store modest treasures and powders.

Plate 129
Pedro Linares.
Alebriges.
Mexico, D.F.
1968.
Papier-mâché, paint and varnish,
approximately 17 X 14 X 19".
SAMA.

Pedro Linares, Mexico's foremost
legendary *cartonero,* created *alebriges:* flying dragons, winged
lizards and mythical creatures that
leap and soar in a world of ultimate
fantasy. As a gravely ill young man,
Linares had a vision in which he
saw ugly and frightening things—
ominous clouds in the shape of
dragons with sharp teeth and pro-
truding eyes hurling themselves at
him. From this trip into eternity
alebriges were born. He transformed
his vision into exuberant paper
monsters that were intricately
painted and wildly outlandish. It is
more likely that Linares, a *cartonero*
by trade, saw a turn-of-the-century
Posada engraving portraying the
seven deadly sins as flying winged
creatures attacking a rich man who
reputedly died as a victim of his
own vices. Linares was fascinated
with the endless artistic potential
of this subject and probably needed
a change from his seasonal production of *piñatas,* Judas figures, devils,
demons and skeletons. With various molds used interchangeably he
creates a large cast of fabulous flying sculptures—each piece is
unique. The three *alebriges* that
Rockefeller owned, made in 1968,
are very early examples of these fantastic Linares works.

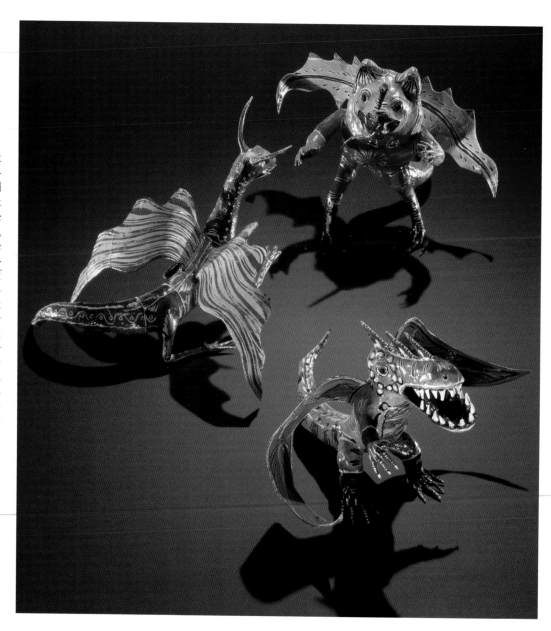

Plate 130
Cart and Animals.
San Martín Tilcajete, Oaxaca.
1970s.
Painted wood and sisal;
cart: 17 X 10 X 11"; oxen: 11 x 7";
tiger: 13 X 5 X 6". SAMA.

Driving through the Valley of Oaxaca, one always sees carts pulled by teams of oxen. They carry enormous loads of wheat, corn and other crops to the pueblos from the fields.

This miniature version of the cart is quite realistic with the exception of the cargo: two oversize men restraining a tiger placed there to make a humorous photograph. The carts always appear to be enormous hand-built toys with very basic construction and joinery making them easy to load and unload. The oxen yoke is a miniature of one Rockefeller bought in the Ocotlán market, where beasts of burden and other animals are sold and bartered.

San Martín Tilcajete has become an important center for carvers in the Oaxaca valley. They developed this craft following the success of Manuel Jiménez.

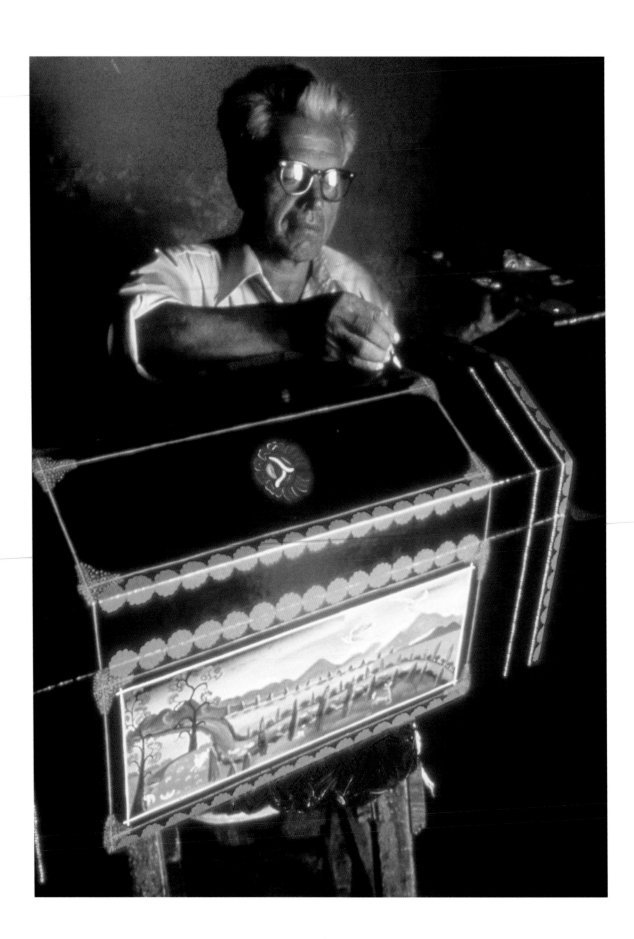

The Mexican Folk Artist

Their hands model the face of Mexico.

—Rafael Carillo Aspeitia[1]

From his first trip to Mexico in 1933 to his last visit in 1978, Rockefeller always was profoundly moved by the creativity of the folk artists he encountered. He never lost sight of the human hand and social history involved in each piece that he collected. His photographic recall of pieces he had discovered nearly fifty years earlier brought back a wealth of memories of remote villages, marketplaces and artisans.

Folk artists are still found all over Mexico. They live and work in the bustling cities, regional market towns and in thousands of small peasant villages throughout the republic. They are young and old, male and female, mestizo and Indian. They are almost always desperately poor. Despite their low economic status, these artists frequently are shown great respect, mainly because they are recognized as vital links between the past and the present and are able to fit important traditional customs into contemporary settings.[2] For the outside world, folk artists are "brokers" of Mexican culture and are largely responsible for presenting images of Mexico as varied as the country itself.

Since Mexican folk artists play to many different audiences and respond to a wide variety of needs, their art is enormously diverse, ranging from the mundane to the exotic, from the ephemeral to the enduring. It is eaten, paraded, broken intentionally, worshiped, adorned, cursed and burned. "Their objects elicit fear, loathing, love, humor, anger, hate, envy and a host of other feelings. They always demand and usually receive strong emotional

Alfonso Jiménez, contemporary Olinalá lacquerware artist, decorating a chest. The stylized pastoral landscape shows a fish-filled river surrounded by rabbits and deer (now mainly hunted out). Doves fly overhead as men work and rest nearby; the rugged mountains surrounding Olinalé are seen in the distance. It takes an artist several weeks to decorate a chest such as this one. Olinalá, Guerrero, 1976.

participation."[3] Although incorrectly described as being detached from their work aesthetically, Mexican folk artists, like all artists, place strong value on their art and are concerned with its effect on others.

Dr. Atl, a pioneer in the study of Mexican folk art and himself a painter, describes some of the anguish of creation in the life of the potter Zacarías Jimón:

> *Ascetic, with large bones, strong hands and jutting jaw, with a wide mouth and features that express continuous concentration. He tells me "I paint because there is something inside that makes me produce in travail . . . my own wish is that I could give away the pots I decorate instead of selling them. One's hands are tied when a piece is commissioned. This thing that is a painting should remain a thing meant for one only, so that whoever likes what has been done may carry it away free."[4]*

Since most folk artists live in close-knit communities, amid those who buy and use their products, they are constantly subject to local criticism. Just as the work of Aztec folk artists reflected upon their moral lives and reputations within the community, the same judgments are often levied upon contemporary folk artists. A weaver whose cloth is loose and uneven will be judged as having a disorganized life. A potter who makes objects that are not balanced is likely to be out of balance in other ways. By contrast, a good folk artist is someone who is in harmony with himself and the surrounding world.

Anxieties over "doing the job right" are also commonly vented by folk artists in Mexico. Consider a traditional artisan from Patamban, Michoacán, who makes paper-thin wax floral arrangements for the church:

> *As the day approaches, and as I am getting behind in my work, I start worrying and can't sleep. In the middle of the night I think up an arch. Should the top be pointed or squared off? Should the circles on the sides be larger or smaller? In my mind I make the changes, then I go back to my original design, and then I start making changes all over again.[5]*

Most folk artists in Mexico today are part-time specialists who spend most of their time carrying out duties not related directly to folk art production. Many are peasant farmers who spend their days in the fields. Some are herdsmen, housewives, carpenters, brick masons and other tradesmen. Mask-maker Javier Olivares, for example, works as postmaster in the small Nahuatl-speaking village of Atliaca, Guerrero, and from time to time he picks up extra money working in a nearby brick factory. For these part-time specialists, folk art offers an escape from a tedious and monotonous lifestyle and an opportunity to express devotion to a saint, to vent frustrations and to supplement meager incomes. More important, it is a way for people of modest incomes to participate in the ceremonial and ritual life of the community through traditionally accepted means. Most often, these artists produce objects for local consumption and frequently for no cost. Their motivation derives from the desire to please a village saint or to satisfy the wishes of their children and the needs of their community. For the most part very conservative artistically, these artists adhere closely to traditional forms and generally work within the boundaries of acceptability established by the community.[6]

Other Mexican folk artists are full-time specialists who use their craft as a main source of financial support for themselves and their families. Herón Martínez, the famous potter from Acatlán, Puebla, is a good example of this type of artist. In some cases, these artists evolved from part-time specialists primarily for economic reasons. Generally, they have a broader world view than their part-time relatives. Their motivation is largely economic, and their artistic response is mainly to a market outside their local area. In the Valley of Oaxaca, folk artists who once responded almost exclusively to local needs are now producing items almost exclusively for outsiders. It is highly probable that folk artists such as woodcarver Manuel Jiménez and the Aguilar family of ceramists have not made folk art for Mexican consumption in years, much less for use in their own small communities. Instead, their highly original objects are sold to foreign visitors or shipped to shops all over the world.

Both of these groups are folk artists, although they are working for different reasons and motivated in different ways. For the first group, motivation is local, strongly traditional and accurately reflects the values and standards of the community in which they live and work. The second group is motivated to a great extent by external economic forces and have

Pedro Linares, of Mexico City, decorating one of his *alebriges*, 1976. Finished and unfinished paper figures in every corner and on every surface give the room a fantastical aura, reflecting the full range of Linares' creativity.

Manuel Jiménez, woodcarver of Arrazola in the Valley of Oaxáca, carving one of his wooden animals, 1977. After carving the animals out of poplar or cedar wood, Jiménez paints them with vivid dyes. Rockefeller collected many of his pieces, which unfortunately were destroyed by insects while in storage.

more readily adapted their work to meet outside demands. Both groups exemplify how folk art is used as a mechanism to cope with social, religious and economic conditions and pressures inside and outside the community.[7]

Folk artists draw their inspiration from the world around them and therefore can provide insightful clues to the nonmaterial culture of the area. Candelario Medrano, the late eccentric figural ceramist from Jalisco, explained:

> *The animals come from stories that my grandmother and grandfather told me when I was an* escuincle *(small child). The yellow animal with the lumpy mane and* metates *(grinding stones) and* petates *(mats) sticking to its side is a bad* nahual *(spirit). During the day it is a person, but at night it turns into a witch and steals things from peoples' kitchens.*[8]

Josefina Aguilar of Ocotlán de Morelos, Oaxaca, and her family draw inspiration from the rites of passage in their small village to create the colorful ceramic weddings, religious processions and funerals for which they are now famous worldwide.

Josefina Aguilar of Ocotlán painting one of her clay dolls, 1977.

Frequently, there is a strong division of labor among folk artists, especially in Indian Mexico. Women who care for children and maintain the household while their husbands work in the fields often engage in folk art activities such as pottery production and weaving, both of which can be done within a family's courtyard. Traditionally, women have always woven on back-strap looms, but in communities where Spanish upright looms are used, weaving is done more frequently by men. In the Nahua community of Zacualpa, Guerrero, pottery production is shared by both sexes, but certain steps of production are performed exclusively by either men or women. Zacualpan men gather the clay and wood for firing, and the women do the actual forming, burnishing and firing. Both men and women take pottery to market to sell.[9]

Mexican folk artists learn their art and skills from a variety of sources. Some folk artists are self-taught, but the incidence of this seems to be rare. In more traditional communities, folk art skills are passed on from mother to daughter, father to son. Children begin to learn the crafts of their parents

An Aguilar child at work on a small figure, Ocotlán, 1977. Children of artisans begin working as soon as they can manipulate the material comfortably.

early, sometimes making practice pieces as soon as they can manipulate the medium. Unlike our own society, in which children's activities differ greatly in kind from those of their parents, in rural Mexico, the difference is mainly one of degree. A child who is learning a craft is not expected to do adult-level production but is expected to engage in the same activity. As the child grows older, expectations rise. One weaver from the Tzotzil village of San Pedro Chenalho, Chiapas, recalls her own socialization as a folk artist:

> *When I was about fifteen, I began to use the spindle . . . . "Do it this way," my mother would say. "Don't make it too soft or too hard." When my spindle didn't turn right she would hit me with it . . . . My mother would say, "Where did you come from, woman, that you don't know how to handle your spindle? Women have to learn. You'll probably have a strict mother-in-law who knows how to weave very well and she'll scold you. She'll hit you on the head with the spindle and whorl if you don't know how to use them."[10]*

In other cases, folk art socialization takes place through lengthy apprenticeship. Candelario Medrano credits his folk skills to his tutelage with folk artist Julio Acero:

> *When I was a little boy I was adopted by Julio Acero, the best toymaker in Santa Cruz. The Señor taught me to make toy whistles, animals and roosters. Before dawn during the month before big holidays, I would take the Señor's burro to get the clay nearby. When I returned, I would spread the clay on the street in front of the Señor's house. In this way, with one day's street traffic, the clay would be broken down enough that by the next morning it could be sifted and mixed with water for the day's clay supply. To this day some potters still place their fresh clay from nearby mines in the street to be broken down by cars and trucks, as well as by foot and cart traffic.*
>
> *The wet clay I mixed first with my bare feet and worked in small sections by kneading it with my hands. The Señor taught me to form the figures of people and animals by hand. The faces we made with old molds which the Señor's father had used before him. When we finished making the figures, we put them inside to dry slowly in the shade. We used to use leña (firewood) and ocote (highly resinous pine chips that burn clean) for fueling the kiln, but now we use dried cow manure and old rubber tires to fire the clay for one or two hours. Yes, the wood is very scarce and expensive now.[11]*

An important and unexplored area of folk art socialization is that which takes place through regional jails. All over Mexico, prisoners must pay for a large portion of their own keep and often do so through the production of folk art, an activity that is learned within the jail from other inmates. Prisoners in Tlapa, Guerrero, make baskets and rush-covered bottles; those in jail in Tehuantepec, Oaxaca, weave hammocks in a style made famous in that area. As early as the late nineteenth century, prisoners in the colonial jail of San Juan de Ulúa, Veracruz, were expertly carving finely detailed scenes on coconut shells. Often these magnificent objects were used as ex-votos depicting the prisoner's crime and showing an appeal to a saint or the Virgin for forgiveness. In some cases, artistic knowledge acquired while in jail is taken back to one's village, where it is introduced and becomes a significant factor in the local folk art scene and economy.

The hands of a Tlaxiaco woman weaving a basket, October 1978.

Folk art is often called "anonymous" art, since most traditional folk artists prefer not to sign their names to their work, either because they simply cannot do so or, more likely, because it is not customary. Members of an artist's community, however, easily pick out the work of individual artists by the way facial features are executed, the formation of handles on the sides of a pot or the manner in which paint is applied to the surface of a gourd. Although no written signatures are usually present, pieces are signed in other ways, allowing them to be identified community-wide as the work of a particular artist.[12]

Although the Mexican folk artist is under constant siege by an increasingly industrialized society that belches forth mass-produced, impersonal objects twenty-four hours a day, they have been amazingly tenacious. While plastics replace clay, synthetic fibers are woven instead of natural ones and tinsel sequins instead of berries and seeds are applied to costumes, folk artists in Mexico continue to interact vigorously with the society in which they live and in their own unique ways chronicle their time for us to enjoy. Perhaps more than any other group, they mold, carve and paint the face of Mexico.

Notes

ROCKEFELLER THE COLLECTOR

1. Douglas Newton, *Masterpieces in Primitive Art* (New York: Alfred A. Knopf, 1978), p. 20.

2. Joe Alex Morris, *Nelson Rockefeller: A Biography* (New York: Harper and Row, 1960), p. 75.

3. Nelson A. Rockefeller, "The Governor Lectures on Art," *The New York Times Magazine*, 9 April 1967.

4. *Masterpieces of Modern Art* (New York: Hudson Hills Press, 1981), p. 13.

5. Bland Blackford, *Bassett Hall, the Williamsburg Home of the Rockefeller Family* (Williamsburg: The Colonial Williamsburg Foundation, 1984), p. 24.

6. Morris, *Rockefeller: A Biography, p.* 73.

7. Abby Aldrich Rockefeller to Nelson A. Rockefeller, 1928, Rockefeller Archive Center, North Tarrytown, N.Y.

8. Mexican Arts Association, Inc., Certificate of Incorporation, Rockefeller Archive Center, North Tarrytown, N.Y.

9. Ibid.

10. *Masterpieces of Modern Art*, p. 5.

11. Francine du Plessix, "Anatomy of a Collector: Nelson Rockefeller," *Art in America* 2 (1965), p. 44.

12. Ibid.

13. Bertram D. Wolfe, *The Fabulous Life of Diego Rivera* (New York: Stein and Day, 1969), p. 302.

14. Ibid., p. 311.

15. Ibid., p. 323.

16. Nelson A. Rockefeller to Diego Rivera, April 1933, Rockefeller Archive Center, North Tarrytown, N.Y.

17. Wolfe, *Fabulous Life of Diego Rivera, p.* 322.

18. Rockefeller, "The Governor Lectures on Art."

19. Rockefeller to Rivera, April 1933, Rockefeller Archive Center.

20. Amy Conger, *Edward Weston in Mexico, 1923–26* (Albuquerque: University of New Mexico Press, 1983), p. 21.

21. Edward Weston, *The Daybooks*, ed. Nancy Newhall, 2 vols. (Millerton, N.Y.: Aperture, 1973), Vol. I, p. 187.

22. Daniel Rubín de la Borbolla, *Arte Popular Mexicano* (Mexico: Fondo de Cultura Económica, 1974), p. 274.

23. Frances Toor, *Mexican Popular Arts* (Mexico: Frances Toor Studios, 1939), p. 11.

24. Weston, *Daybooks*, Vol. I, p. 130.

25. Telephone interview with Sarah d'Harnoncourt, 25 March 1987.

26. Weston, *Daybooks*, Vol. I, p. 172.

27. Jean Charlot, *The Mexican Mural Renaissance, 1920–1921* (New Haven: Yale University Press, 1963), p. 29.

28. René d'Harnoncourt, *Mexican Arts* (Portland, Maine: Southworth Press, 1930), p. XI.

29. Interview with Mildred Constantine, April 1987, New York.

30. Ibid.

31. Charles R. Richards to Thomas B. Appleget, 23 May 1928, Rockefeller Archive Center, North Tarrytown, N.Y.

32. Newton, *Masterpieces in Primitive Art*, p. 20.

33. Essay by Rockefeller, November 1978, Rockefeller Archive Center, North Tarrytown, N.Y. Previously unpublished, this essay now appears in its entirety as the Foreword of this book, pp. xxiii–xxix.

34. Ibid.

35. Ibid.

36. William Spratling, *File on Spratling: An Autobiography* (Boston: Little, Brown, 1967).

37. Carlos Espejel, *The Nelson A. Rockefeller Collection of Mexican Folk Art* (San Francisco: Chronicle Books and the Mexican Museum, 1986), p. 3.

38. Ibid.

39. Interview with Mary C. Rockefeller, New York, April 1987.

40. Espejel, *Rockefeller Collection of Mexican Folk Art*, p. 3.

41. Carl Fox, *The Nelson A. Rockefeller Collection of Mexican Folk Art* (New York: The Museum of Primitive Art, 1969).

42. Wolfe, *Fabulous Life of Diego Rivera*, p. 377.

43. Essay by Rockefeller, November 1978. See note 32.

44. Ibid.

45. Ibid.

46. Du Plessix, "Anatomy of a Collector," p. 27.

47. Rockefeller to Rivera, April 1933, Rockefeller Archive Center.

48. Ibid.

49. Newton, *Masterpieces in Primitive Art*, p. 19.

50. James R. Mellow, "Rocky as a Collector," *The New York Times Magazine*, 18 May 1969.

51. Interview with Laurance Rockefeller, New York, April 1987.

52. Du Plessix, "Anatomy of a Collector," p. 27.

53. Ibid., p. 46.

54. Ibid., p. 27.

55. Malcolm N. Carter, "Nelson Rockefeller: 'I know exactly what I like,'" *ARTnews*, May 1978, p. 115.

56. Espejel, *Rockefeller Collection of Mexican Folk Art*, p. 4.

THE COLLECTION

1. Katherine Anne Porter, *Outline of Mexican Arts and Crafts* (Los Angeles: Young and McCallister, 1922), p. 4.

2. Nelson A. Rockefeller to Robert C. Smith, 6 July 1942, Rockefeller Archive Center, North Tarrytown, N. Y.

3. Interview with Susan Herter, Santa Fe, Spring 1987.

4. 20 *Centuries of Mexican Art* (New York: The Museum of Modern Art and the Instituto Nacional de Antropología e Historia, 1940); Carl Fox, *The Nelson A. Rockefeller Collection of Mexican Folk Art* (New York: The Museum of Primitive Art, 1969); Annie O'Neill and Charlene Cerny, *Mexican Folk Art from the Collection of Nelson A. Rockefeller* (New York: Center for Inter-American Relations, 1984); Carlos Espejel, *The Nelson A. Rockefeller Collection of Mexican Folk Art* (San Francisco: Chronicle Books and the Mexican Museum, 1986); and Marion Oettinger, Jr., *Con Cariño: Mexican Folk Art from the Collection of the San Antonio Museum Association* (San Antonio: San Antonio Museum Association, 1986).

5. Frances Toor's 1939 catalogue, *Mexican Popular Arts*, has a photograph of Tulimán pottery taken by Manuel Alvarez Bravo, p. 64.

6. The Robert K. Winn collection of Mexican folk art in San Antonio contains a similar object. Unfortunately, it, too, is without certain provenance.

7. For a good discussion of Mexican furniture, see *El Mueble Mexicano: Historia, Evolución e Influencia* by Carmen Aguilera et al. (Mexico: Fomento Cultural Banamex, 1985).

8. Leopoldo Méndez et al., *The Ephemeral and the Eternal of Mexican Folk Art,* 2 vols. (Mexico: Fondo Editorial de la Plástica Mexicana, 1971), Vol. I, p. 335.

9. An excellent discussion of the history, description and use of the sarape can be found in Ramón Mena's article "El Zarape," *Mexican Magazine* 4, Vol. II (September 1926).

10. James Jeter and Paula Marie Juelke, *The Saltillo Sarape* (Santa Barbara: New World Arts, 1978).

11. Chloë Sayer, *Costumes of Mexico* (Austin: The University of Texas Press, 1985), p. 51.

12. Méndez et al., *Ephemeral and Eternal*, Vol. II, p. 738.

13. Ibid., p. 739.

14. Annie O'Neill and Charlene Cerny, *Mexican Folk Art from the Collection of Nelson A. Rockefeller* (New York: Center for Inter-American Relations, 1984), p. 13.

15. Méndez et al., *Ephemeral and Eternal*, Vol. I, p. 337.

16. O'Neill and Cerny, *Mexican Folk Art*, p. 29.

17. Francisco Javier Hernández, *El Juguete Popular en México: Estudio de Interpretación* (Mexico: Ediciones Mexicanas, 1950).

18. Roberto Montenegro, *Museo de Artes Populares* (Mexico: Ediciones de Arte, 1948), p. 29.

19. Weston, *Daybooks*, Vol. I, pp. 172–73.

20. Jorge Enciso, "Painting on Wood in Michoacán and Guerrero," *Mexican Folkways* 1, Vol. VIII (1933), pp. 4–34.

THE MEXICAN FOLK ARTIST

1. Méndez et al., *Ephemeral and Eternal*, Vol. I, p. 10.

2. Marion Oettinger, Jr., *Con Cariño: Mexican Folk Art from the Collection of the San Antonio Museum Association* (San Antonio: San Antonio Museum Association, 1986), p. 27.

3. Ibid.

4. Charlot, *Mexican Mural Renaissance*, p. 28.

5. Fernando Horcasitas, "Mexican Folk Art," *National Geographic* 5, vol. 153, p. 654.

6. Oettinger, Jr., *Con Cariño*, p. 27.

7. Ibid., p. 28.

8. Lenore Hoag Mulryan, *Mexican Figural Ceramicists and Their Works* (Los Angeles: Museum of Cultural History, UCLA, 1982), p. 19.

9. Marion Oettinger, Jr., and Ted Warmbold, *Zacualpa Ceramics: Traditional Pottery from Southern Mexico* (San Antonio: San Antonio Museum Association, 1986).

10. Sayer, *Costumes of Mexico*, pp. 130–31.

11. Mulryan, *Mexican Figural Ceramicists*, pp. 17–18.

12. Oettinger, Jr., *Con Cariño*, p. 28.

Chronology

1908	Nelson A. Rockefeller born in Bar Harbor, Maine, on July 8, the third of five children, to John Davison Rockefeller, Jr., and Abby Aldrich Rockefeller.
1918-26	Attends Lincoln School, New York City.
1926-30	Attends Dartmouth College, graduating with a degree in economics. Elected to Phi Beta Kappa.
1930	Returns to New York to enter family businesses.
1930-31	Travels around the world. Meets Rosa and Miguel Covarrubias in Bali. Develops an interest in primitive and popular art and collects his first objects.
1932	Elected to Board of Trustees at the Metropolitan Museum of Art. Takes an active role in the Museum of Modern Art. Diego Rivera's Rockefeller Center mural project begins and is terminated.
1933	First trip to Mexico to buy paintings for the Museum of Modern Art generates what will become a lifelong interest in Mexican popular and pre-Hispanic art. While there, visits archaeological sites and the remote countryside; is introduced to Roberto Montenegro, William Spratling, Fred Davis, Frances Flynn Paine and David Alfaro Siqueiros; and buys twenty-six cases of popular and pre-Hispanic art.
Mid-1930s	Meets René d'Harnoncourt, who becomes his mentor in collecting.
1935	Becomes a director of Creole Petroleum, a Venezuelan-based oil company.
1937	Takes first trip to Peru; brings back a planeload of weavings and artifacts. Takes a twenty-nation tour of Latin America to study economic, social and political conditions.
1938	Made president of Rockefeller Center.
1939	Travels again in Latin America. Elected president of Museum of Modern Art; begins planning the first major show of Mexican culture in the United States.
1940	Helps organize a major exhibition, *20 Centuries of Mexican Art,* at the Museum of Modern Art. Becomes coordinator of the Office of Inter-American Affairs, which he established at the request of President Roosevelt. Resigns his directorship in Creole Petroleum. Organizes Rockefeller Brothers Fund, with his four brothers. Serves as American co-chairman of the Mexican-American Development Commission.
1944	Appointed Assistant Secretary of State for American Republic Affairs by President Roosevelt.

1945	Initiates the first Inter-American Conference of Problems of War and Peace, known as the Chapultepec Conference, held in Mexico City. Resigns as Assistant Secretary of State for American Republic Affairs. Active in the establishment of the United Nations.
1946	Becomes chairman of the board of Rockefeller Center. Receives Order of the Aztec Eagle from the Mexican government. Rockefeller Brothers establishes the American International Association for Economic and Social Development (AIA), which finances many nonprofit health, educational, agricultural and social projects in Latin America.
1947	Organizes International Basic Economy Corporation (IBEC) to help raise living standards in foreign countries through new economic enterprises, concentrating initially in Latin America.
1948	Travels to Mexico in June with his family; Roberto Montenegro accompanies Rockefellers.
1954	Founds Museum of Primitive Art in New York with René d'Harnoncourt. (The museum opened in 1957.)
1959	Becomes governor of New York State. Is eventually elected to four four-year terms.
1960	Creates the nation's first State Council on the Arts.
1969	Exhibition of Rockefeller's Mexican folk art collection opens at the Museum of Primitive Art, New York. This is the first time the material has been shown in twenty-five years.
1973	Resigns as governor of New York State.
1974-77	Holds office of vice president of the United States under President Gerald R. Ford.
1977	Returns to Rockefeller family office in New York City.
1978	Embarks on a series of five art books on his major collections. Begins Nelson Rockefeller Collections, a business to reproduce major works from his collections. Travels to Oaxaca, Mexico, to reacquaint himself with Mexico and its folk art. Begins work on book about his Mexican folk art collection.
1979	Dies January 27, of a heart attack.

Glossary

Abrazo. An embrace between males in Latin America. A form of greeting

Alebriges. Fantastic papier-mâché figures made by the family of Pedro Linares. Probably inspired by a woodcut by José Guadalupe Posada

Ambiente. Physical or spiritual environment in which a thing is found

Banderillero. One who sticks *banderillas* (darts) into a bull's nape prior to the kill

Barrio. A distinct ward or neighborhood of a city or town

Bolsa. Bag or purse

Calavera. Skull

Campesino. A peasant or one who lives in the *campo* (countryside) and works the land

Cántaro. Water jug

Cargador. Porter or person who carries things

Charreada. Mexican rodeo in which *charros* perform

Charro. Mexican horseback riders who perform cowboy stunts

Colonias. Ward or barrio of a town

Concha. Guitar used by *conchero* dancers. Back of most of these guitars is made of armadillo shell

Conchero. Dancer who dresses in romantic Aztec attire and usually performs at major pilgrimage sites and on feast days

Copal. Incense made from pine resin, used in religious ceremonies throughout Mexico

Escuincle. Derived from the Nahuatl word for "dog," used as a term of endearment for children

Estofado. Technique of decorating sculpture whereby the carving is covered with plaster and painted and adorned with gold leaf

Ex-voto. A votive offering, most frequently in the form of a painting placed on an altar to commemorate recovery from a grave illness or escape from serious danger. Very popular in nineteenth-century Mexico

Faja. A belt or sash

Hacienda. Large rural estate

Huipil.	A straight, sleeveless and shapeless blouse of pre-Hispanic origin still worn by Indian women in some parts of Mexico
Huitzilopochtli.	Aztec god of war
Ikat.	A method of textile decoration in which select threads are wrapped and thereby separated prior to dyeing
Ixtle.	Fiber from the maguey plant, used primarily to make bags and nets
Juguete.	Toy
Leña.	Firewood
Lináloe.	A scented wood, rare today, used in lacquerware of Olinalá, Guerrero
Lotería.	Lottery game similar to Bingo
Matador.	Bullfighter
Matraca.	Noisemaker frequently used during Carnival and on Saturday of Glory during Holy Week
Mercado.	Marketplace, as well as the activities occurring there
Mestizo.	A person of mixed blood, usually Spanish and Indian. Also a cultural indicator
Metate.	Grinding stone
Milagro.	Miracle. Also name of miniature objects in silver, tin and gold pinned on or near a religious image as an offering for a favor, such as miniature eyes for problems of sight, ears for hearing difficulties and countless other forms, still used in churches throughout Mexico
Morral.	Bag
Nahual.	One's spiritual counterpart. Often an animal and frequently mischievous
Ocote.	Resinous wood used to start fires and make torches
Olla.	A clay cooking pot
Petate.	A woven palm mat used for sleeping
Picador.	Horseman who spears bull in nape to lower the head in a bullfight
Popote.	Mexican straw used for making brooms
Portal.	Portico
Promesa.	A religious pledge
Pulque.	A slightly alcoholic drink, made from the maguey plant, whose use dates to pre-Hispanic times

Pulquería.	A place where pulque is sold and consumed, frequently decorated with murals, altars and other forms of folk expression
Quechquémitl.	A triangular shoulder garment of pre-Hispanic origin, still worn by Indian women in some parts of Mexico
Raffia.	A type of palm fiber used in the weaving of mats and baskets
Rebozo.	A multipurpose shawl worn by women in rural Mexico
Retablo.	A religious screen behind the altar. Also, paintings of saints and other religious figures placed behind church and household altars. Frequently painted on tin or copper
Sarape.	A rectangular garment with slit opening for head. Worn mainly by males
Sombrero.	A large hat
Tabla.	A board, or when used in reference to Huichol art, a large panel
Tastoane.	Masked dancer (and dance) related to Santiago (Saint James) and historical battles between Christians and Moors. Found in the State of Jalisco
Tequitqui.	Works of art during the Spanish colonial period, which continued to show survivals of indigenous style
Tlaloc.	Aztec god of rain
Toro.	Bull
Tortilla.	A round flat bread made of corn or, less frequently, of flour. Basic diet of rural Mexico
Velación.	Vigil

Bibliography

Aguilera, Carmen, et al. *El Mueble Mexicano: Historia, Evolución e Influencia*. Mexico: Fomento Cultural Banamex, 1985.

Atl, Dr. [Gerardo Murillo]. *Las Artes Populares en México*. 2 vols. Mexico: Editorial Cultura, 1921.

Blackford, Bland. *Bassett Hall, the Williamsburg Home of the Rockefeller Family*. Williamsburg: The Colonial Williamsburg Foundation, 1984.

Bullock, William. *Six Months' Residence and Travels in Mexico*. London: John Murray, 1824.

Calderón de la Barca, Frances. *Life in Mexico: The Letters of Fanny Calderón de la Barca*. Garden City: Doubleday, 1966.

Carter, Malcolm N. "Nelson Rockefeller: 'I know exactly what I like.'" *ARTnews*, May 1978.

Cerny, Charlene. "Everyday Masterpieces." *The New York Times*, n.d.

Charlot, Jean. *The Mexican Mural Renaissance, 1920–1921*. New Haven: Yale University Press, 1963.

Codex Mendoza. Mexico: 1979.

Collier, Peter, and David Horowitz. *The Rockefellers: An American Dynasty*. New York: Holt, Rinehart and Winston, 1976.

Conger, Amy. *Edward Weston in Mexico, 1923–26*. Albuquerque: University of New Mexico Press, 1983.

Decaen (ed. pub.). *México y sus alrededores. Colección de vistas, trajes y monumentos*. Mexico, 1855–56.

Du Plessix, Francine. "Anatomy of a Collector: Nelson Rockefeller." *Art in America* 2 (1965).

Durán, Fray Diego. *Book of the Gods and Rite of the Ancient Calendar*. Norman: The University of Oklahoma Press, 1971.

Eche, Tseng Yu-Ho. *Chinese Folk Art in American Collections*. The Chinese Institute of America, 1976.

Enciso, Jorge. "Painting on Wood in Michoacán and Guerrero." *Mexican Folkways* 1, vol. VIII (1933).

Erb, Charles. *Nelson A. Rockefeller and Latin America*. N.d.

Espejel, Carlos. *Mexican Folk Crafts*. Barcelona: Editorial Blume, 1978.

_____. *Mexican Popular Ceramics.* Barcelona: Editorial Blume, 1975.

_____. *The Nelson A. Rockefeller Collection of Mexican Folk Art.* San Francisco: Chronicle Books and the Mexican Museum, 1986.

_____. *Olinalá.* Mexico, D.F.: SEP-INI, Museo Nacional de Artes e Industrias Populares, 1976.

Esser, Janet Brody. *Máscaras Ceremoniales de los Tarascos de la Sierra de Michoacán.* Mexico City: Instituto Nacional Indigenista, 1984.

_____. "The Persistent Memory: New Directions in Folk Art Studies." *Arte Vivo: Living Traditions in Mexican Folk Art.* Memphis: Memphis State University Gallery, 1984.

Fomento Cultural Banamex. *Mexico: XIX Century People and Landscapes.* Mexico: Fomento Cultural Banamex, 1981.

Fox, Carl. *The Nelson A. Rockefeller Collection of Mexican Folk Art.* New York: The Museum of Primitive Art, 1969.

Harnoncourt, René d'. *Mexican Arts.* Portland, Maine: Southworth Press, 1930.

Hernández, Francisco Javier. *El Juguete Popular en México: Estudio de Interpretación.* Mexico: Ediciones Mexicanas, 1950.

Herrera, Hayden. *Frida.* New York: Harper and Row, 1983.

Horcasitas, Fernando. "Mexican Folk Art." *National Geographic* 5, vol. 153 (1978).

Jeter, James, and Paula Marie Juelke. *The Saltillo Sarape.* Santa Barbara: New World Arts, 1978.

Kelemen, Pál. *Vanishing Art of the Americas.* New York: Walker and Company, 1977.

Linati, Claudis. *Costumes civils, militaires et religieux du Mexique.* Brussels, 1828.

Masterpieces of Modern Art. New York: Hudson Hills Press, 1981.

Mellow, James R. "*Rocky as a Collector.*" *The New York Times Magazine,* 18 May 1969.

Mena, Ramón. "*El Zarape.*" *Mexican Magazine* 4, vol. II (September 1926).

Méndez, Leopoldo, et al. *The Ephemeral and the Eternal of Mexican Folk Art.* 2 vols. Mexico: Fondo Editorial de la Plástica Mexicana, 1971.

Montenegro, Roberto. *Museo de Artes Populares.* Mexico: Ediciones de Arte, 1948.

Morris, Joe Alex. *Nelson Rockefeller: A Biography.* New York: Harper and Row, 1960.

Mulryan, Lenore Hoag. *Mexican Figural Ceramicists and Their Works.* Los Angeles: Museum of Cultural History, UCLA, 1982.

Navarrete, Carlos. "Prohibición de la danza del tigre." *Tlalocan,* vol. VI, no. 4 (1971).

Nebel, Carlos. *Voyage pittoresque et archeologique dans la partie la plus interéssante du Mexique.* Paris, 1836.

Newton, Douglas. *Masterpieces in Primitive Art.* New York: Alfred A. Knopf, 1978

Oettinger, Marion, Jr. *Con Cariño: Mexican Folk Art from the Collection of the San Antonio Museum Association.* San Antonio: San Antonio Museum Association, 1986.

_____. *Dancing Faces. Mexican Masks in a Cultural Context.* Washington, D. C.: Meridian House International, 1985.

_____, and Ted Warmbold. *Zacualpa Ceramics: Traditional Pottery from Southern Mexico.* San Antonio: San Antonio Museum Association, 1986.

O'Neill, Annie. "Nelson A. Rockefeller: The Collector." In Carlos Espejel, *The Nelson A. Rockefeller Collection of Mexican Folk Art.* San Francisco: Chronicle Books and the Mexican Museum, 1986.

_____, and Charlene Cerny. *Mexican Folk Art from the Collection of Nelson A. Rockefeller.* New York: Center for Inter-American Relations, 1984.

Porter, Katherine Anne. *Outline of Mexican Arts and Crafts.* Los Angeles: Young and Mc-Callister, 1922.

Redfield, Robert. *Peasant Society and Culture.* Chicago: The University of Chicago Press, 1956.

Richard, Paul. "Gentle Strokes from Gentle Folks." *The Washington Post,* 19 November 1981.

Rockefeller, Nelson A. "The Governor Lectures on Art." *The New York Times Magazine,* 9 April 1967.

Rockefeller Report on the Americas. Chicago: Quadrangle Books, 1969.

Rubín de la Borbolla, Daniel. *Arte Popular Mexicano.* Mexico: Fondo de Cultura Económica, 1974.

Saarinen, Aline. *The Proud Possessors.* New York: Random House, 1958.

Sahagún, Fray Bernardino de. *General History of the Things of New Spain (Florentine Codex),* Book 10. Santa Fe: The School of American Research, 1961.

Sayer, Chloë. *Costumes of Mexico.* Austin: The University of Texas Press, 1985.

Spratling, William. *File on Spratling: An Autobiography.* Boston: Little, Brown, 1967.

Starr, Frederick. *Catalogue of a Collection of Objects Illustrating the Folklore of Mexico.* London: The Folklore Society, 1898.

Teshe, Robert T. "What Is Folk Art?" *El Palacio,* vol. 88 (1982–83).

Toor, Frances. *Mexican Popular Arts.* Mexico: Frances Toor Studios, 1939.

_____. *A Treasury of Mexican Folkways.* New York: Crown, 1947.

20 Centuries of Mexican Art. New York: The Museum of Modern Art and the Instituto Nacional de Antropología e Historia, 1940.

Walz, W. G. *Illustrated Catalogue of Mexican Art Goods and Curiosities.* Philadelphia: Edward Stern, 1888.

Ward, H. G. *Mexico in 1827.* 2 vols. London, 1828.

Weismann, Elizabeth Wilder. *Art and Time in Mexico.* New York: Harper and Row, 1985.

Weston, Edward. *The Daybooks.* 2 vols. Edited and introduced by Nancy Newhall. Millerton, N.Y.: Aperture, 1973.

Wolf, Eric. *Sons of the Shaking Earth.* Chicago: The University of Chicago Press, n.d.

Wolfe, Bertram D. *The Fabulous Life of Diego Rivera.* New York: Stein and Day, 1969.

Index

Photograph Credits

The photographs of the objects (which are designated as plates) were taken by Lee Boltin, unless otherwise noted below:
John Dyer: plates 7, 9–11, 13, 14, 37, 40, 52, 54, 60, 65–69, 74, 84, 86, 88, 89, 93, 94, 97, 10 1, 105, 110, 119, 120, 123, 125; Steve Tucker: plates 62, 124.

Credits for all other photographs appear below (numbers refer to page numbers):
Courtesy Mexican Museum, San Francisco: xlii; Annie O'Neill: xvi, xvii, xviii, xxii, xxvi, xxx, xxxiv, xxxv, 27, 33, 161, 163, 164, 165, 169; Nelson A. Rockefeller: xxv, xxvii, xxviii, 30; Courtesy Rockefeller Archive Center: 4, 17, 20, 21, 23; Charles Uht: 24, 25.